MACHINE GUNS OF WORLD WAR I

LIVE FIRING CLASSIC MILITARY WEAPONS IN COLOUR PHOTOGRAPHS

MACHINE GUNS OF WORLD WAR I

ROBERT BRUCE

Windrow & Greene

This edition published in Great Britain 1997 by Windrow & Greene Ltd 5 Gerrard Street London W1V 7LJ

Designed by Frank Ainscough Printed by BOOKBUILDERS LTD

A CIP catalogue record for this book is available from the British Library

ISBN 1 85915 078 0

Author's Preface

The mission of this second book in Windrow & Greene's *Live Firing* series is not only to give readers a brief historical account of the principal automatic weapons of the Great War; but - centrally - to convey for those who will probably never have an opportunity to handle such firearms themselves the practical experience of actually preparing and firing these oddly configured and often complicated weapons. Each chapter is built around photography of an actual live firing session conducted in the USA by experienced shooters, and includes close-ups of handling, stripping, loading and firing. We have taken pains to observe and document every weapon from an infantryman's point of view: to find out how well it loads and fires; how difficult it is to control and shoot accurately; what eccentricities it may have; and how suitable it was for the tactical purpose intended by official doctrine at the time.

We have made considerable efforts to depict these weapons realistically, as if encountered on the Western Front of 1914-18. We apologise that this has not always been possible in exact detail; the long subsequent life of some of these much-developed weapons has introduced a few unavoidable anachronisms which we have tried to acknowledge (alert and knowledgeable readers will no doubt hasten to point out others, and constructive advice will be welcomed). The same is true of some of the period uniforms with which our shooters were provided; but even if not museum-perfect in every detail, we believe they are valuable in giving a convincing visual context to the period weapons.

It is with greatest appreciation that we acknowledge the assistance of the shooters pictured here, and many others who provided guns, uniforms, ammunition, accessories, research and technical advice. While specific credit is given at the end of each chapter, it usually doesn't end there. Many of these same names can be found acknowledged in the modern reference books listed in the Bibliography. They have unselfishly shared the fruits of countless hours of study and practical expertise, so that a body of unique experience will not die as these guns become increasingly rare - and there is a real danger that this knowledge will be lost in some oppressive future, as misguided officials thwart Constitutional guarantees in order to confiscate these functioning museum pieces from their rightful caretakers and destroy them under the guise of public safety.

Many of the people who unselfishly contributed their time and knowledge to this project are historical re-enactors, "living history" enthusiasts who feel a deep respect and kinship for those brave men whose courage and sacrifice in the mud, wire, filth and fire of the old Western Front is almost unimaginable today. Through this endeavour it is hoped that readers of today's generation may come to have some slight idea of what superhuman effort it took not only to survive but to fight and win, with and against machine guns, in that shell-blasted hell on earth.

CONTENTS

INTRODUCTION

All the guns examined here belong to the class known as "automatic": i.e. they are capable of mechanically reloading themselves through the action of firing, and will continue shooting uninterrupted as long as the trigger is held and ammunition is fed into the action. Although in popular American parlance these are generically termed "machine guns", they actually comprise three distinct categories: machine pistols, firing pistol calibre ammunition; machine rifles/ automatic rifles/ light machine guns, firing rifle calibre ammunition and having rifle-type stocks for shoulder firing; and true machine guns, firing standard or special high powered rifle ammunition and mounted on a tripod.

Though necessarily not arranged in exact chronological order, the separate historical accounts in this book may be said to have a continuous connecting story. It begins with the huge impact on infantry warfare of the tripod-mounted machine gun as used by soldiers of the German, British, French, and American armies in the Great War. It continues with the changes to their principal gun forced on the Germans by the tactical realities of trench warfare; with the Allies' introduction of simpler, lighter weapons in response to the same pressures; and with the consequent transformation of infantry minor tactics. It ends with the appearance late in the war of a radical new machine pistol or sub-machine gun, as a trench-clearing weapon for Germany's elite "storm troops" - the most effective manifestation of that transformation of tactics.

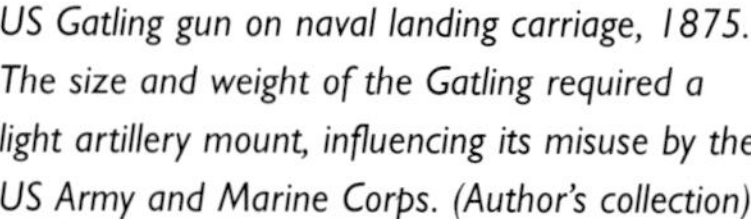

US Gatling gun on naval landing carriage, 1875. The size and weight of the Gatling required a light artillery mount, influencing its misuse by the US Army and Marine Corps. (Author's collection)

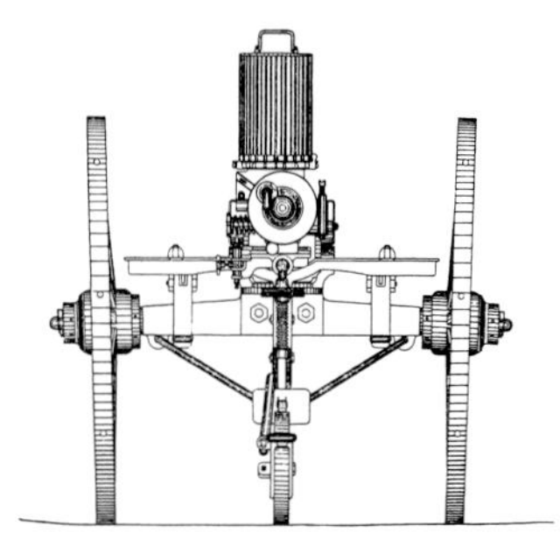

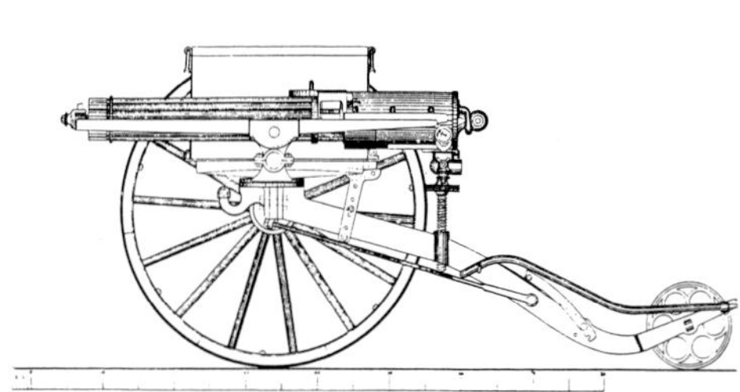

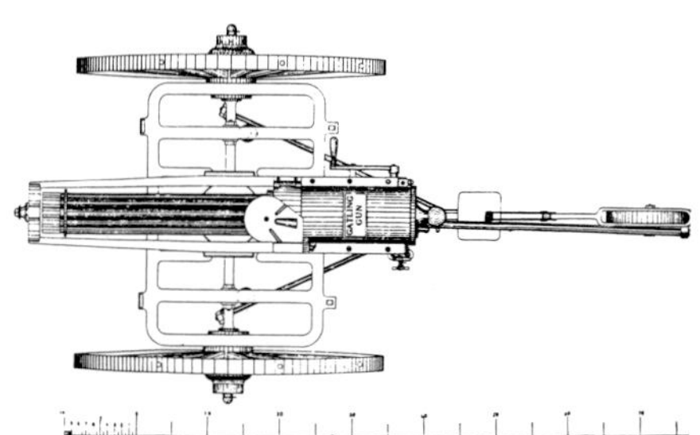

The background: man-powered machine guns

By the time the European powers began their four year duel to the death, repeating guns fired by various hopper-fed, hand-cranked systems had already been in widespread military service for some 50 years. While many of these were both technically clumsy and poorly employed by tacticians, all showed great ingenuity in the search for ways to increase firepower without increasing manpower. American inventor Dr.Richard Gatling's hand-cranked gun with multiple revolving barrels - the best known of these - was first used against Confederate forces during the siege of Petersburg in 1864. It went on to achieve some degree of fame in the Spanish-American War of 1898 (enthusiastically championed in the disdainful and hidebound US Army by one Lt.John "Machine Gun" Parker), and was used to some extent by the British in colonial campaigns.

Other notable examples were the Gardner and the Nordenfeldt. The first, invented in 1874 by former Union Army officer William Gardner and soon manufactured by Pratt & Whitney, initially had two breech-loading barrels whose rounds were loaded, fired, and ejected by a single turn of a hand crank. While unable to interest the US Army in his gun, Gardner found willing customers in the British Army and Royal Navy. The inferior Nordenfeldt's main patents were registered in 1878; designed by Swedish engineer Heldge Palmcrantz, it was vigorously (and unscrupulously) marketed by banker Thorsten Nordenfeldt.

The Maxim system

It was another American inventor, Hiram Stevens Maxim, who first dispensed with hand cranking, instead initiating the cycle of operation by harnessing the recoil force generated by each exploding cartridge. In April 1885, in a demonstration for the British Institute of Mechanical Engineers of his "automatic machine gun", Maxim stood nearly motionless to unleash a continuous torrent of lead as .45in black powder rifle cartridges in a long canvas belt were flawlessly ingested and fired. Maxim's gun introduced Industrial Age efficiency to the nasty job of battlefield slaughter. Much more than just a labour-saving device for soldiers, his gun was a fraction of the size and weight of most of its contemporaries. One weapon, occupying a few feet of space and attended by a handful of men, could do the same job as a 50-man platoon of riflemen.

Maxims were acquired by the British and used with differing fortunes in various colonial campaigns, beginning with an expedition in Matabeleland in 1893; and in time Hiram Maxim would be knighted for his services to the British Empire. The Maxim "toggle joint" lock and related parts were simplified over the years, resulting in the superlative British Vickers gun adopted in 1912.

Principal cartridges used by automatic weapons of World War I (left to right): German 9mm Parabellum (Luger) ball; 7.92mm Mauser ball; 7.92mm Mauser wooden-tipped blank; French 8mm Lebel ball; British .303in Mk VII ball. Note that the German cartridges have "rimless" cases, and the French and British rounds very prominent rims. This is a major factor for designers of automatic weapon ammunition delivery, feeding and extraction systems.

Tactical trial and error

The obvious technical advance represented by Maxim's guns quickly led to their proliferation among European powers; but it would be years before an effective tactical doctrine was worked out for their open field use. They were successfully used for the point defence of, e.g., colonial forts; but the instinct of the military authorities was to try to integrate them into the existing tactical manoeuvres of large forces of infantry, cavalry and artillery. The lesson of France's mistake in trying to use her *mitrailleuses* volley guns as "light artillery" in the Franco-Prussian War of 1870 had not yet been fully digested. Both sides in the Boer War (1899-1902) used Maxims - indeed, the Boers also had 37mm automatic cannon or "pom-poms", which outranged British machine guns and seriously "got on the nerves" of those subjected to their fire; but no major tactical innovations emerged.

For a clear-sighted judgement of the machine gun's true potential in a conventional war between two modern armies we must look to an article on the Russo-Japanese War in Manchuria (1904-05) in the June 1908 issue of *Militar Wochenblatt*, quoted by Maj.F.V.Longstaff and Capt.A.H.Atteridge in their indespensible work *The Book of the Machine Gun* (1917). In this conflict the Tsar's forces were well equipped with water-cooled Maxims, and the Japanese skillfully employed air-cooled Hotchkiss guns:

"The machine guns were extraordinarily successful. In the defence of entrenchments especially they had a most telling effect on the assailants at the moment of the assault. But they were also of service to the attack, being extremely useful in sweeping the crest of the defenders' parapets; as a few men can advance under cover with these weapons during an engagement, it is possible to bring them up without much loss to a decisive point. The fire of six machine guns is equal to that of a battalion, and this is of enormous importance at the decisive moment and place."

An early five-barrel model of the American Gardner hand-cranked machine gun, c.1885; note that each barrel has its own gravity-feed cartridge rack above the receiver. (Author's collection)

The final version of the Gardner, in naval service; this has a single barrel enclosed by a water cooling jacket. (US Army Center for Military History - USACMH)

LEFT *Engraving from an early picture showing Hiram Maxim (in top hat) demonstrating his machine gun to the explorer and newspaperman Henry M.Stanley (seated); note the empties piled up in front of the gun. (Courtesy Dover Pictorial Archive)*

The 37mm Maxim "Pom-Pom" in service with the Boers during the South African War, 1899-1902; note (right) the belt of heavy shells. (From Das Maxim Maschinengewehr und seine Verwendung *von Hauptmann Braunn, Berlin, 1903: USACMH)*

Russian crew, c.1915, with Maxim on armoured field carriage as also used during the Russo-Japanese War. (NARA)

Manchuria, c.1905: Japanese Hotchkiss on armour-shielded tripod - a photo taken by US Army observer Capt.John J.Pershing, later the commanding general of the AEF. The Japanese Army successfully used Hotchkiss guns for both direct and indirect fire in their war with Russia. (From *Military Intelligence: A Pictorial History.*)

Meanwhile, inventors all over Europe and America were hard at work turning out machine guns in a variety of forms. With patent laws locking up all aspects of the Gatling, Maxim, Hotchkiss and other guns, some interesting alternatives were found to established methods of feeding, firing, and cooling. Once again in North America - seemingly the garden of machine gun genius - John Moses Browning had successfully developed his Colt Model 1895, an air-cooled, belt-fed weapon whose action was cycled by a swinging piston arm mounted under the barrel. (This distinctive feature earned it the nickname "Potato Digger" from its resemblance to that piece of agricultural machinery.) Simpler and cheaper than the Maxim, the Colt achieved wide commercial success; it was belatedly adopted by the US Army, and was used on American fighter airplanes during the World War as the Colt-Marlin Models 1917 and 1918, with its gas system modified to a more conventional piston configuration. (Several of the weapons examined in their ground-fighting role in this book were the subject of interesting modifications for use as fixed or flexible armament on aircraft; but aerial gunnery is another story, and space forbids their inclusion here.)

Another American, Laurence Benet, working in France at the Hotchkiss factory established by his fellow-countryman Benjamin Hotchkiss, collaborated with Frenchman Henri Mercié to produce the Fusil Mitrailleur Mle 1909. Intended as a more compact and portable supplement to the tripod-mounted Hotchkiss, this weapon was adopted by the US Army that same year as the Benet-Mercié Machine Rifle Model 1909; and in 1916, in .303in calibre, by the British Army, where it was popularly known as the "Portative" . Although a clever simplification of the highly successful Hotchkiss Mle 1900, it was not entirely satisfactory, and in British service was issued only to the cavalry.

Altogether more original and significant was the first light machine rifle to be fed from a detachable box magazine. The Danish Madsen 8mm Rekytgavaer M1903 proved an excellent weapon for cavalry and light infantry; although not officially adopted by the primary belligerents in the World War, its developed models were bought in great numbers by the Germans and used by Alpine and assault troops.

The Science of Machine Gunnery

"The machine-guns were enfilading our men from La Boiselle, and from the high ground above the bullets came pattering down in showers, so that when they hit men in the shoulder they came out at the wrist. They swept No Man's Land like a scythe." Thus a young British infantry officer, quoted by war correspondent Philip Gibbs in his 1917 book *The Battles of the Somme*.

There is a lingering popular misconception about the way machine guns are used in conventional warfare. Contrary to the image presented in countless war movies, these bullet-hoses are not all that efficient when fired head-on into a line of advancing troops. In the early months of the Great War they were certainly used to horrendous effect, cutting down like rows of corn those enemies who were foolhardy enough to advance on them in frontal attacks. But, as the casualty-producing limitations of even the most thorough preparatory artillery barrages became more fully understood by commanders, intentional instances of such suicidally brave folly became increasingly rare. Knowing that they would be crossing a shell-blasted wasteland under interlocking fields of fire from well hidden enemy machine guns, attacking troops of both sides soon learned that short rushes from one hole to another were more productive.

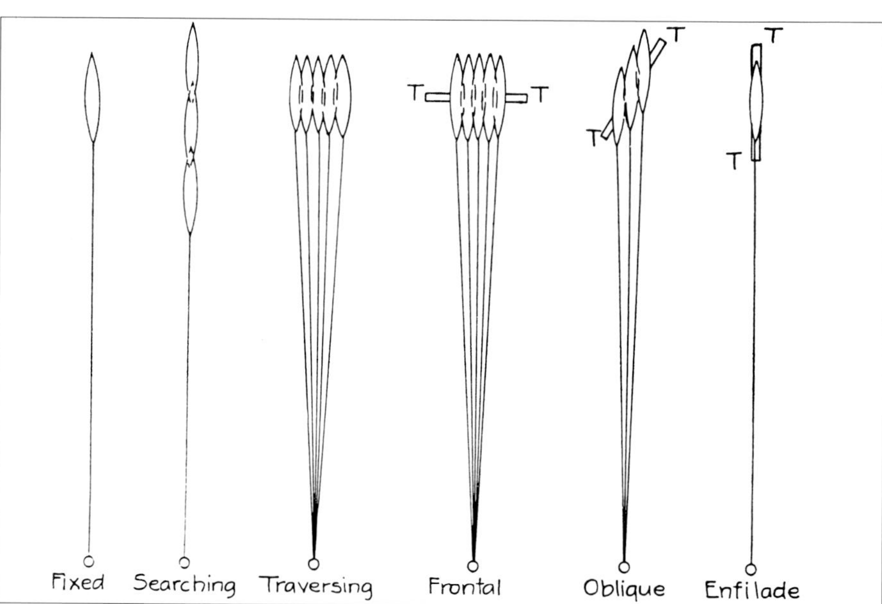

RIGHT *Orders given to machine gun crews might include specific tasks calling for "searching" or other types of fire illustrated here. ROTC manual, 1925. (Author's collection)*

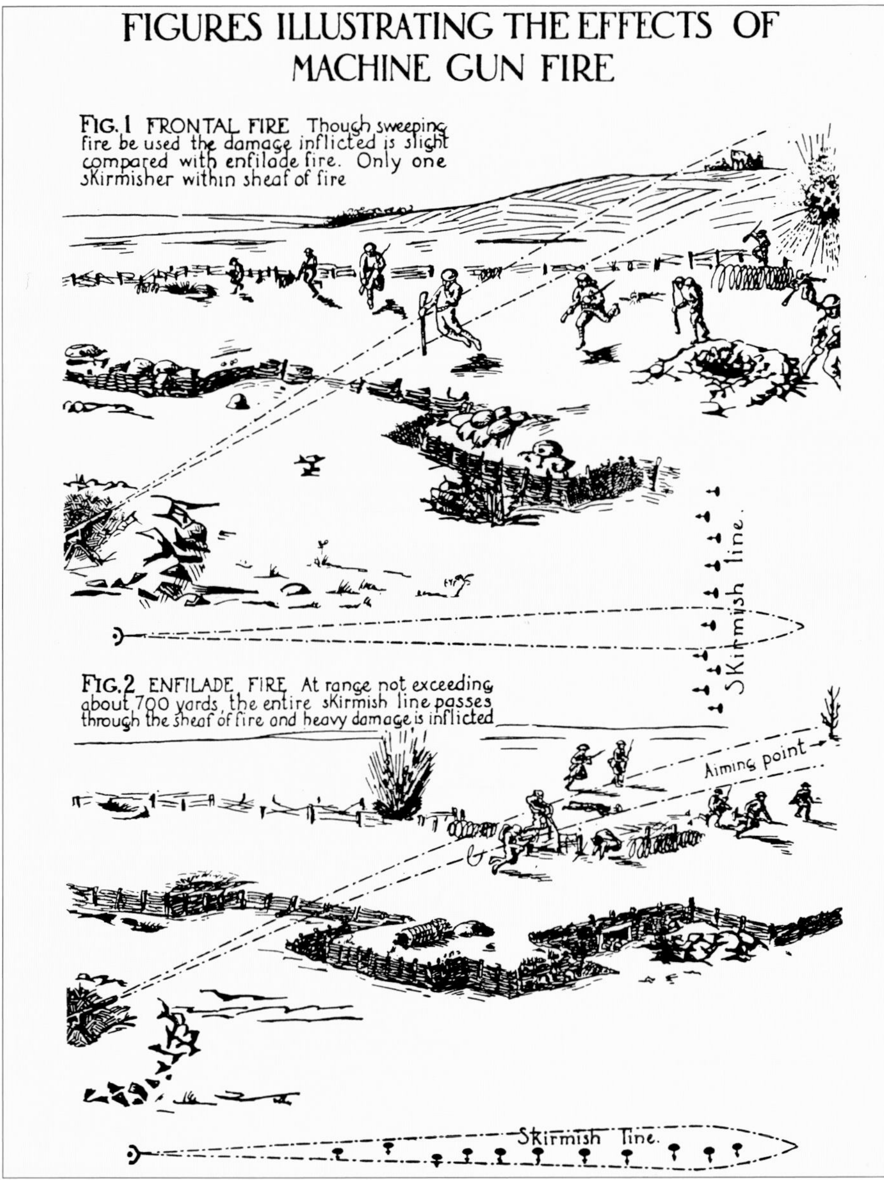

Enfilade fire is the most effective, since the long axis of the target coincides with the long axis of the beaten zone; "all parts of the beaten zone fall on the target and, due to the depth of the beaten zone, a considerable part of the target is covered by one burst". To take advantage of natural dispersion of each burst of fire, it is desirable to determine the enemy's most likely avenue of approach and then place the guns on their flanks. This allows the oval-shaped beaten zone of each burst to fall onto a larger number of attackers. With carefully placed barbed wire, assault troops could be channeled into interlocking fields of fire and cut down with murderous precision. ROTC manual, 1925. (Author's collection)

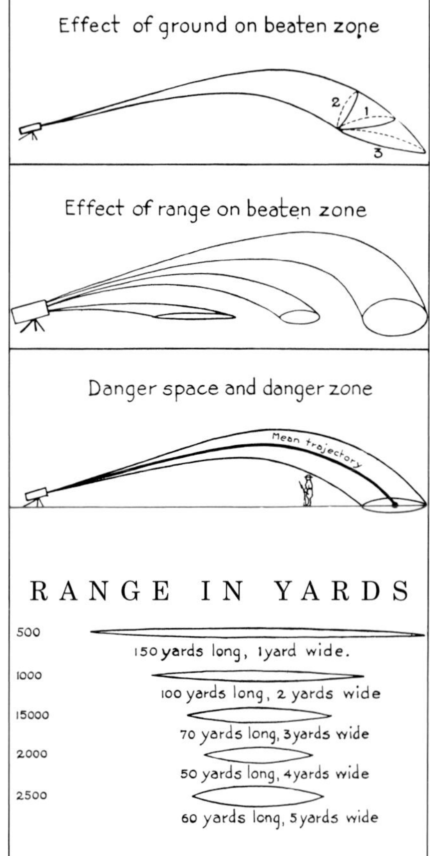

The effects of concentrated machine gun fire; each burst forms a "beaten zone" of bullets, whose shape changes with the slope of the ground, the trajectory and the range - e.g. it changes from narrow to wide with increasing range. The greatest lethality is achieved when the beaten zone can be placed to fall over the greatest number of troops: "The gunner must know the dimensions of the effective beaten zone. . . and fit it to his target. . .The danger space along the line from the gun to the point of strike of the lowest shot is that within which a standing man would be hit." ROTC manual, 1925. (Author's collection)

The theory and practical applications of machine gun fire have been minutely examined and recorded; the source used here is the 1925 edition of National Service Publishing Company's *Reserve Officer Training Course, 1st Year Advanced, Vol.III* - just one example of the accumulated wisdom of the Great War years. To any professional soldier or serious student this sort of detailed, specific technical material is fascinating; sadly, pressure of space and a mercilessly philistine editor prevent extensive quotation, but the diagrams reproduced here may be instructive as far as they go.

These refer to "direct laying" - aimed fire at visible targets; but the same principles applied to the serious job of overhead and indirect fire. Heavy machine guns were capable of safely delivering fire over the heads of advancing friendly troops because of their fixed mounts and small overhead dispersion. Because of the danger of killing one's own troops, this task was approached with the utmost deliberation and care.

Indirect fire

To the uninitiated modern reader, perhaps the most surprising aspect of Great War machine gunnery is the importance placed on indirect fire - that is, the science of delivering fire onto targets beyond visual range. Indirect fire is far more difficult to carry out properly, but it can be almost diabolical in its effectiveness. Its chief virtue is in allowing guns safely positioned well behind friendly lines to bring murderous fire on the enemy, using the same aiming methods and geometric calculations as artillery, but with quite a different effect. Instead of being warned by the scream or whistle of an incoming artillery round, victims of a long range machine gun barrage often heard nothing more than a stirring as of wind in the grass, followed by the thud of bodies being hit and the screams of the wounded and dying. The horror of this situation must have been extraordinary:

"Usually one or two guns would do a little strafing every night: simply going out into the field in front of the building and setting up the gun in a convenient

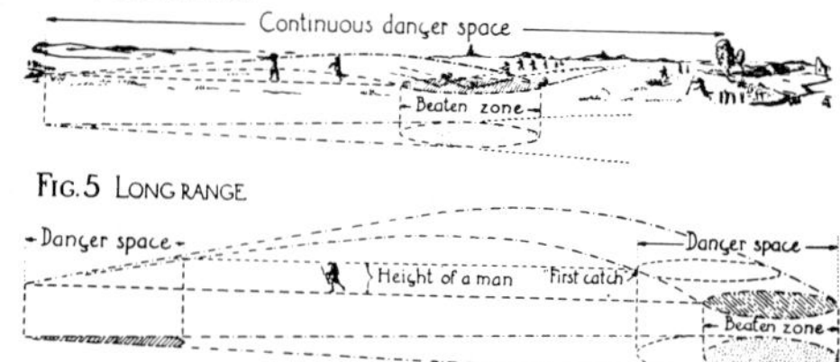

Obviously, the "danger space" includes not only the beaten zone but all of the area within the trajectory of each burst, which varies according to the range. ROTC manual, 1925. (Author's collection)

shell-hole. After awhile, from our own observations and from information supplied by the artillery, we occasionally located an enemy battery within range of our guns. Then we would have a regular 'strafing party'. Laying all the guns so as to deliver a converging fire on the battery position, we would, as soon as it was dark, open up on them, knowing that they would be moving about in the open and exposed to fire. We could always tell when we had 'stung' them, for they would invariably come back at us with tremendous fire, shooting wildly at everything within our lines in the vain endeavor to locate us. I'll bet we caused them to expend a hundred thousand rounds of perfectly good ammunition in this way, but we never had a man hit while at the game."

This is from *The Emma Gees* by Capt.Herbert McBride, an officer of the 21st Battalion, Canadian Expeditionary Force; there are countless other stories, from all of the combatant armies, of heavy machine gun units conducting hours-long barrages on their enemies, only to be tormented themselves in turn. Such shoots were laid on to deny the use of otherwise "safe" areas behind the trenches, to harrass and kill on main communications routes and intersections, and to plunge downward at a steep angle into the trenches themselves.

The precise mathematics of indirect fire are too complicated for the scope of this book. By the end of the war a whole catalogue of devices, manuals and tables had been developed to assist with the task of hitting the unseen with the unseeable. These included both standard and surveyor's compasses, clinometers and angle of site instruments, protractors, optical range finders, special binoculars, night firing boxes and aiming posts. They were supplemented with highly accurate large scale maps detailing nearly every mound or ditch in the operational area, and often by high resolution photos taken daily by reconnaissance aircraft. Armed with these tools, a clever officer with the proper Machine Gun School training could - in the only mildly exaggerated words of one seasoned veteran - "shoot fleas off a dog's ear at two thousand yards." Captain McBride again:

"The next day we received an issue of clinometers - quadrants - such as were used by the light artillery. These, together with prismatic compasses, protractors, maps and elevation charts, comprised the firing equipment with which we took the field. There were, of course, numerous and sometimes amazing gadgets being turned out and offered for the purpose of simplifying the problems of the Emma Gee [machine gun] officer, many of them of no practical use and none of them living up to the expectations of the inventors." (From *A Rifleman Went to War*).

In the simplest terms, guns were laid on invisible targets by compass bearing, this being recorded and marked by placing a stake some distance in front of the gun. The angle of elevation appropriate to the desired range, known performance of the gun, type of ammunition, etc. was calculated by using clinometers or angle of sight instruments and mathematical tables. Many of the common requirements for indirect laying of machine guns could be determined using the "Satara Director", one of a number of inspired combinations of clinometer, protractor, and firing tables.

In Britain some Volunteer regiments acquired Maxims and carriages to their own chosen specifications; and various experimental models were seen in small numbers, including this light, air-cooled Maxim with a folding tripod photographed in c.1898 in a special infantry backpack. (USACMH)

Command and control

Since heavy machine guns were most often employed in groups for maximum effect, things could get complicated as the tactical commander positioned several sections of guns for attack or defence; it was necessary to prepare complex and detailed battery charts, and drawings overlaid on the master map for the sector. Then, the light machine guns used in direct support of the heavy guns and the riflemen had to be positioned and co-ordinated to mesh their relative strengths and weaknesses intelligently.

Finally, the fire of the heavy guns had to be co-ordinated and controlled for maximum effect and to fit in with such critical details as friendly patrols, working parties, attack or defensive action. Seemingly mundane but vital details such as the timely resupply of ammunition had to be arranged; this often led to highly detailed orders specifying when, where, and how much ammunition to shoot. Modifications or cues to these fire missions were also specified, as by field telephone, signal flags or panels, or the urgent launching of colour-coded signal flares for SOS ("save our souls") fire missions to rescue front line infantrymen about to overrun:

"The machine guns of our battalion were distributed in depth. Although all positions had been selected primarily for direct fire over the sights up to ranges of 1000 yards and over, each gun had been, where possible, given an indirect SOS line on to ground in front of our front line." (9th MGC, 21-27 March 1918).

It will be obvious by now to students of post-1918 tactics that these sorts of elaborate plans and restrictions would not work on the fluid battlefield of today; but they were eminently suitable and absolutely necessary for the gridlock of trench warfare in France and Flanders, where the main battle lines hardly changed more than a few miles in nearly four years.

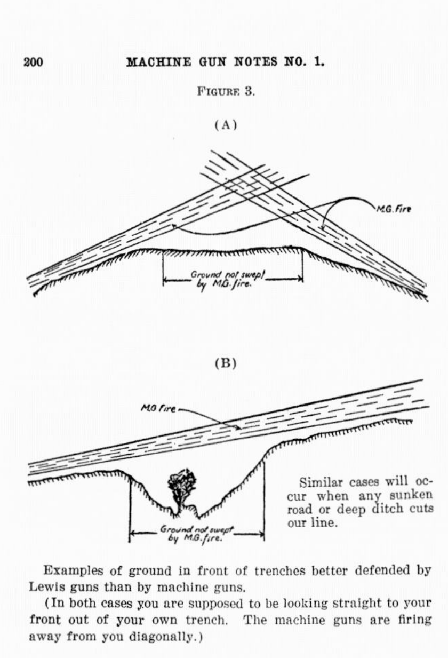
200 **MACHINE GUN NOTES NO. 1.**

FIGURE 3.

(A)

(B)

Similar cases will occur when any sunken road or deep ditch cuts our line.

Examples of ground in front of trenches better defended by Lewis guns than by machine guns.
(In both cases you are supposed to be looking straight to your front out of your own trench. The machine guns are firing away from you diagonally.)

MACHINE GUN NOTES NO. 1. 201

FIGURE 4.

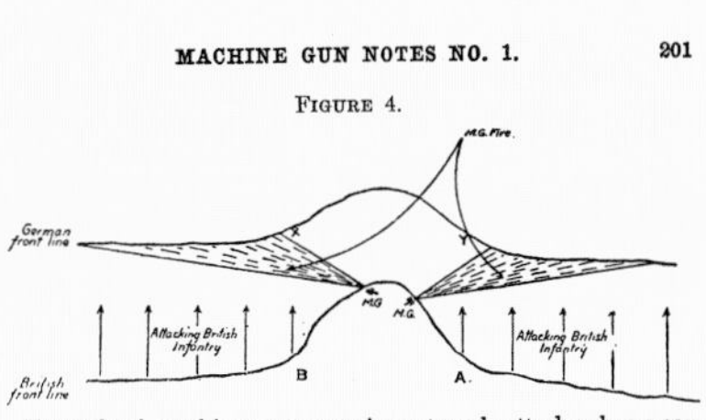

Example of machine guns covering a trench attack, when a gap is left in the line of attack A—B—a British salient. The infantry can get more than half-way across before masking the M.G. fire. The enemy's line must be well bombarded between X—Y, to prevent them from making this a rallying point for reserves, and must be watched by Lewis guns from M.G. emplacements. (Conventional drawing to show arrangement.)

FIGURE 5.

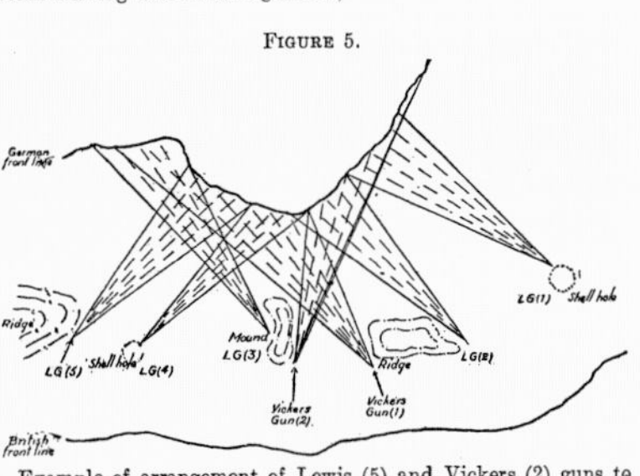

Example of arrangement of Lewis (5) and Vickers (2) guns to cover attack on German salient. The Vickers sweep the whole length of the parapet in their zones. The Lewis guns are allotted sections which they must watch for M.G. emplacements. These are always likely to be found in the sides of a salient.

LEFT *Because of their very different capabilities, tactical commanders gave different but harmonised tasks to the heavy Vickers guns - accurate, long-ranged, and capable of sustained fire - and the light Lewis guns - shorter-ranged, but concealable and quickly movable. This illustration from a 1917 British manual shows how they could work in concert. (Author's collection)*

GUN CHART							Battery A
							Group II
Gun No. 3		Magnetic Azimuth Base Line					565
Task	Clock Time	Time	Gun Angle from Base Line	Q.E.	Traverse	Search	Rate of Fire
A			L 36	84	36	—	125
B			L 310	101	—	—	125
C			L 578	99	—	16	125
Remarks Task A will be fired on Green Star Rocket							

When time allowed an individual gun chart, giving selected information from the battery chart, was prepared for each Vickers gun commander for fire missions. "Task A" here may be a so-called SOS ("save our souls") mission, enfilading a likely avenue of attack and fired if the infantry being covered send up the pre-arranged signal of a green star rocket. ROTC manual, 1925. (Author's collection)

Finally, just a few definitions for terms that will be encountered in this book; most are selectively quoted from the 1918 edition of *Machine Gun Service Regulations*, based on British and French doctrine and published by the US Army's War Plans Division:

Glossary

Barrage (curtain of fire): Ordinarily, direct or indirect fire organised on a large scale - the combined "sheafs" (cones of fire) of two or more guns.
Battery: Guns organised as fire units for barrage work, usually consisting of four to eight guns.
Battle sight: The position of the sight of a gun when the leaf is laid down.
Communication trench: A zigzag ditch leading from the rear to the front line through which reinforcements, reliefs, ammunition and rations were brought up.
Cyclic rate: The rate at which a gun delivers its fire while operating without interruption.
Defilade: An obstacle of sufficient thickness to intercept projectiles and afford shelter from fire delivered at a given point.
Effective beaten zone: The ground beaten by the best 75% of the shots.
Fire control: The exercise of control by a commander over his units enabling him to regulate their fire - pertaining especially to the technicalities immediately involved in delivery of fire.
First catch: Where the lowest shot of the sheaf will first strike an object of given height.
First graze: Where the lowest shot of the sheaf strikes the ground.
Getting sparks: When a bullet struck barbed wire at night it generally threw off a bluish spark; machine gunners used this method to "set" their gun after dark so that its fire would command the enemy's parapet.
Gun chart: Information taken from a Battery Chart prepared for several guns, supplying complete indirect firing data for each gun and its targets for a particular fire mission.
Harassing fire: Directed at assembly points, lines of communication, stores dumps, communication trenches, etc. to interfere with enemy movements and preparations.
Head space: The distance between the face of the bolt and the opening to the chamber. Ideally, this may be precisely adjusted by the gunner to provide just enough support to the base of the cartridge on detonation so as not to allow the rim and base to be blown off.
Night firing box: An illuminated box which permits the sights to be aligned on an aiming mark at night.
Range card: Simple sketch showing direct fire targets and prominent terrain features in relation to the gun position.
Salvo: Battery firing of two or more guns simultaneously.
Sheaf: Imaginary cone containing all the trajectories in a series of shots or burst.
Windage: The influence of the wind in deflecting the bullet from the point of aim; also, the correction necessary to align the sights to the line of the barrel.

Combined clinometer and angle of sight instrument, c.1912. The scale is marked in 10 degrees above (red) and 10 degrees below (black) horizontal; minutes are read off the collars, which are graduated in five-minute intervals. (Author's collection)

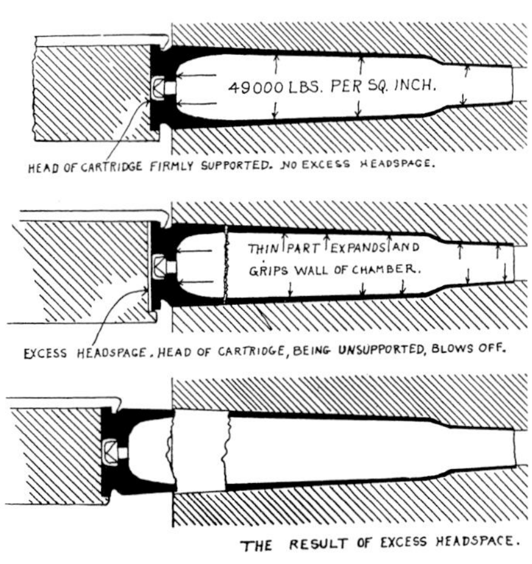

Everybody talks about headspace, but nobody does anything about it ... The Vickers had this provision, the MG 08 did not. (from Machine Guns *by Hatcher – see Bibliography)*

Part of the customary seven-man crew of a German MG08 early in the Great War. Although heavy and complex, the "sled" was a versatile and extremely stable mount for direct and indirect fire. Note the double ammunition box holding 500 rounds, and the gun commander using binoculars to spot targets and correct fire. (US National Archives & Records Administration - NARA)

MAXIM MASCHINENGEWEHR 08

Right side profile the "The Grim Reaper" - our test MG08, a 1917 Spandau-made gun, set up with ammunition and tool boxes.

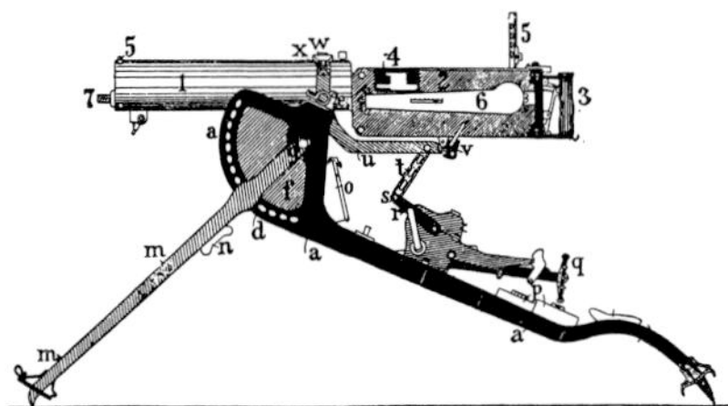

The MG08 and its quadripod with major parts identified: (1) Barrel jacket (2) Receiver (3) "Spade" grip traversing handles (4) Feed block (5) Raised tangent sight (6) Fusee spring housing (7) Muzzle (a) "Sled runner" rear legs (d) Securing catch for front leg adjustment slots (e) Horizontal trunnions for vertical movement (m) Front legs (n) Leather pads for shoulders when mount carried by one man (o) Spare lock stowage (p) Small spares & lubricants stowage (q) Elevating handwheel (r) Locking handle for elevating gear (s) Hinged joint (t) Elevating gear link (u) Mounting frame (v) Locking handle for traversing gear (w) Vertical trunnion for horizontal movement (x) Wingnut securing gun in mounting cradle. (Author's collection)

"The battle of the Somme has again shown the decisive value of machine guns in defence. If they can be kept in a serviceable condition until the enemy's infantry attack, and are then brought up into the firing position in time, every attack must fail. The greater the efforts the enemy makes in the future to destroy our trenches before his assault by an increased expenditure of artillery ammunition, the greater the extent to which we must rely on the employment of machine guns for repulsing attacks. These should be brought into action unexpectedly and continue the fight when the greater part of the garrison of the front-line trenches is out of action and the enemy's barrage fire renders it difficult to bring up reinforcements. Von Hoehn"

(From HQ 6th Bavarian Division, 3 September 1916)

"It was the fire of German machine guns which was most trying for our men. Again and again soldiers have told me today that the hard time came when these bullets began to play upon them. . . A young officer of the Northumberland Fusiliers paid a high tribute to them. 'They are wonderful men,' he said, 'and work their machines until they are bombed to death. In the trenches by Fricourt they stayed on when all other men had either been killed or wounded, and would neither surrender nor escape'."

(Philip Gibbs, *The Battles of the Somme*, 1917)

As the European powers armed themselves against actual and potential enemies at the beginning of the 20th century Hiram Maxim's guns - made and sold by Vickers Sons & Maxim of London - were acquired by all comers as fast as they could be produced. Curiously, the German General Staff were relatively slow to recognise the utility of the machine gun; but their Kaiser was not. Wilhelm II had witnessed a comprehensive field trial of the prominent contenders at Spandau in 1890. When the Maxim easily out-performed the Gatling, Gardner, and Nordenfeldt entries the Kaiser reportedly declared "That is the gun - there is no other!"; what is more, he bought the first few guns for the Guard regiments out of his own pocket.

The adoption of Maxims by rival powers, and reports of their performance from German observers of campaigns in Africa, India and China, soon spurred the General Staff into action. In 1901 a license production agreement for the "Maschinengewehr 01" was obtained by the firm that would become Deutsche Waffen und Munitionsfabriken (DWM) of Berlin, and limited numbers were produced both for German Army use and for export. Detailed manuals were drawn up to standardise crew training and battlefield employment; the concepts explored included direct and indirect fire, pre-zeroed night fire, and overhead support fire.

As early as 1903 eleven Maschinengewehr-Abteilungen (machine gun detachments) had been formed, each of six horse-drawn MG01 guns with ammunition wagons. At first prevailing misconceptions led these guns to be seen as fast, mobile fire support for cavalry units, to provide a base of fire until reinforcements could come up to take an objective. However, the Boer War and the Russo-Japanese War, where conventional artillery easily outranged and destroyed machine guns committed to this "light artillery" role, forced the recognition that the new weapon's tactical future lay with the infantry and in defensive fortifications.

DWM were ordered to lighten the gun and develop a more manageable mount. The resulting MG08 and its elaborate *Schlitten* ("sled") quadripod mount were slightly lightened; curiously, Maxim's original mechanism was essentially untouched, although DWM engineers undoubtedly knew about Vickers' success with an inverted lock mechanism which allowed substantial reduction in receiver size and weight.

OPPOSITE *Reconstruction - Third Battle of Ypres, September 1917: a gunner of a divisional Maschinengewehr-Scharfschuetzen-Abteilung fights on alone, manning an MG08 in a sandbagged emplacement covering the flanks of a hard-pressed infantry battalion. He wears the M1916 helmet, M1917 gas mask, and universal pattern greatcoat of post-1915.*

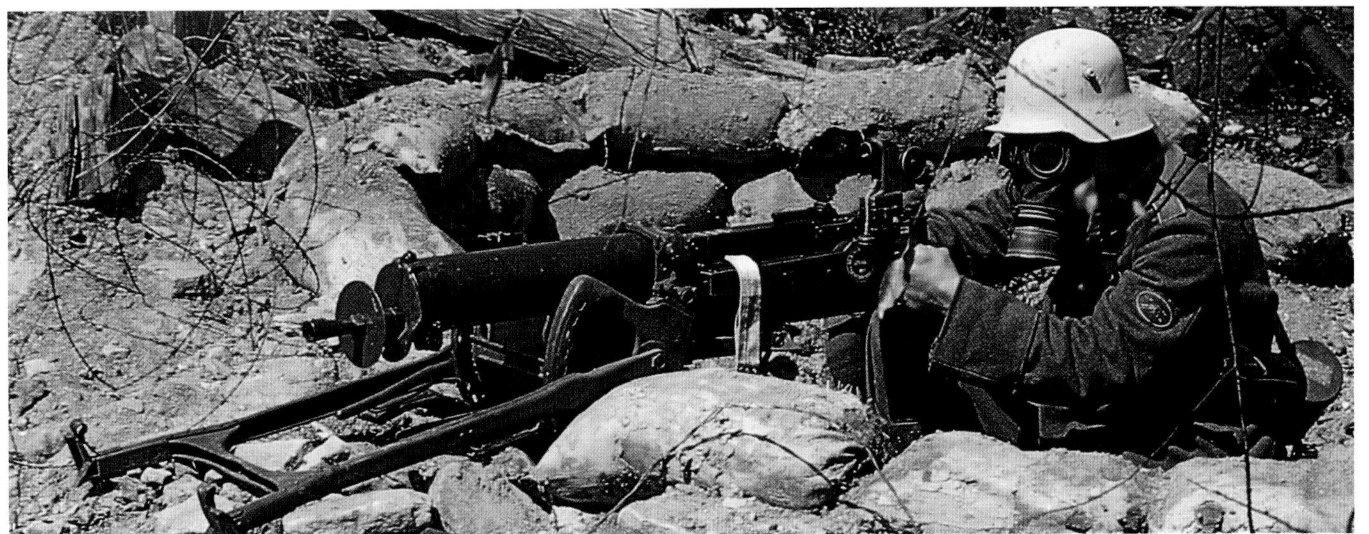

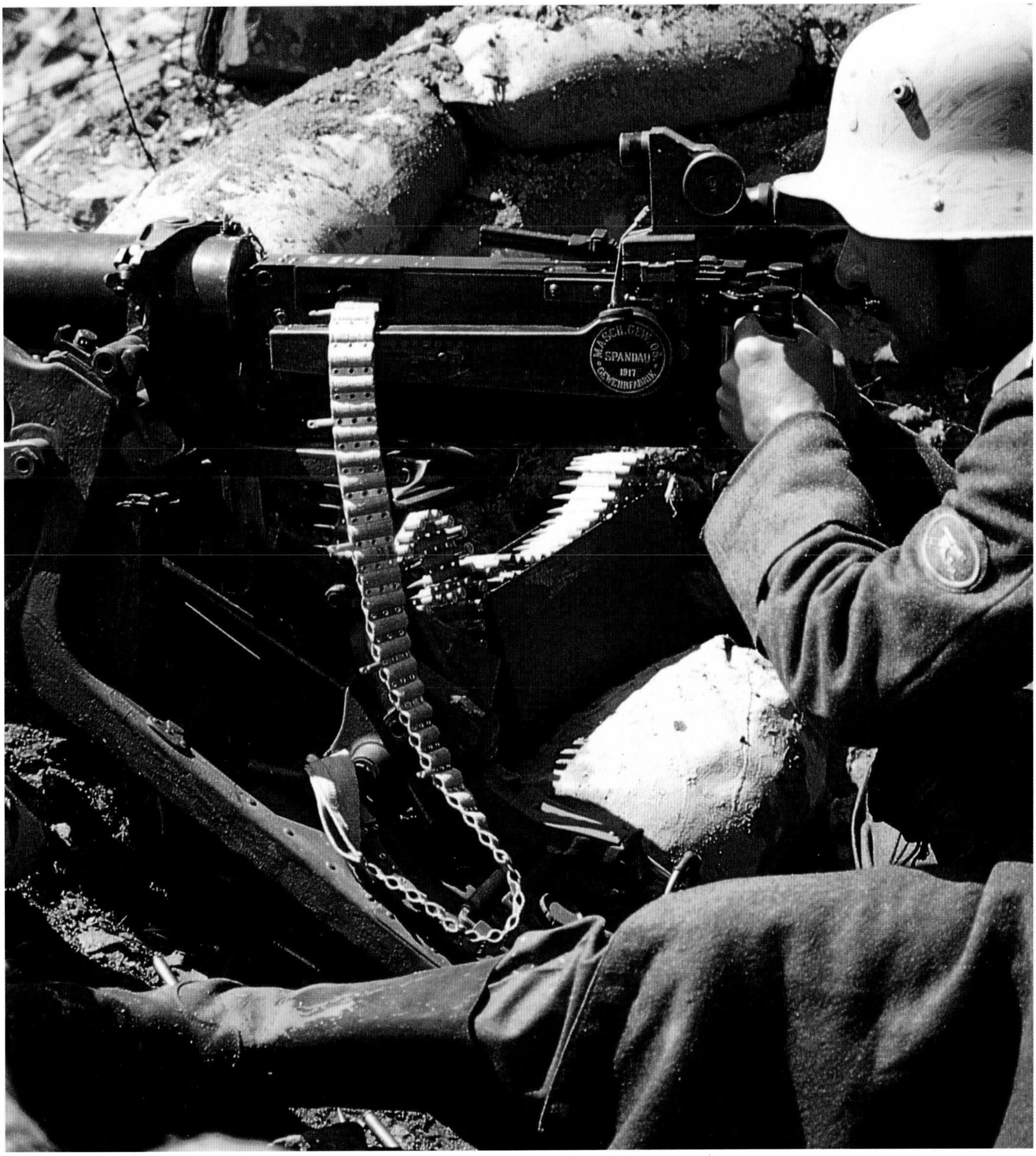
MASCH.GEW.08.
SPANDAU
1917
GEWEHRFABRIK

MG08 gunner with personal equipment; note his holstered "artillery model" long-barrelled Luger pistol, Fernglas 08 binocular case, and gas mask slung in the ready position.

The detail above shows the attachment rings at the ends of the crossed leather dragging straps often seen in contemporary photos of MG crews; these were used to ease manhandling of the gun or heavy ammo chests across country. (Courtesy Daniel Murphy)

"The War to End Wars"

When Germany declared war on France on 3 August 1914, every Jaeger battalion and infantry regiment had a special company with six Maxims - a total in excess of 1,600 guns. No other combatant army could match the Germans' firepower, and the effect on the massed infantry and cavalry assaults of the early months of the war was almost unimaginable. In spite of heavy censorship, newspapers recounted innumerable instances of grisly casualties on both sides. The war of movement congealed, and the opposing battle lines sank into trench networks, where the importance of massed artillery and machine gun fire became obvious to all but the most obstinate generals.

The Germans were quick to grasp that in defence one MG company could often do the work of an entire infantry battalion; and they astutely moved the guns held in reserve up to the front lines, where they were concentrated in dominant positions. In the hysteria of the period, reports of the number of German guns were greatly exaggerated by the press. These inflated figures are still repeated even today, with some references preserving the myth of as many as 25,000 German heavy machine guns in use during the first year of war. Certainly, clever tactical concentration of the Kaiser's 1,600 to 2,000 guns contributed to the carnage and subsequent misinformation.

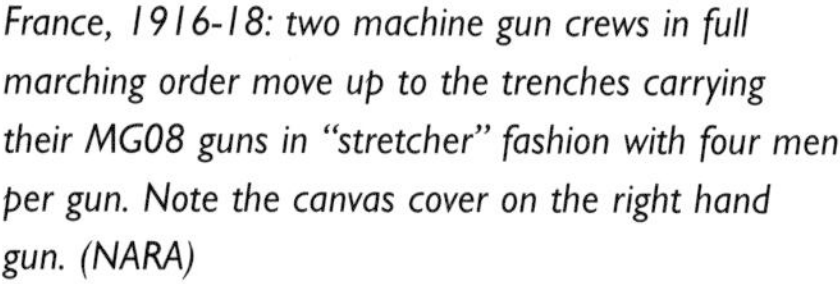

France, 1916-18: two machine gun crews in full marching order move up to the trenches carrying their MG08 guns in "stretcher" fashion with four men per gun. Note the canvas cover on the right hand gun. (NARA)

By 1916 the support elements within each infantry division were standardised. New "Machine Gun Sharpshooter Detachments" each comprised a battalion of three companies, each company consisting of four officers, 133 NCOs and enlisted men, and six MG08 guns. In addition, by late 1916 the infantry unit allocation had been increased to one six-gun company per battalion - 72 per division; so the density of machine guns at the front was indeed formidable. Production of the MG08 increased rapidly during each year of the war, and by the end some 72,000 are said to have been made by DWM and Spandau.

The German Army's MG08 was aimed and fired by the gunner but directed by the gun commander, who was usually an experienced and highly trained NCO. Using a specialised set of binoculars for direct fire missions, he observed bullet strike and called corrections to the gunner. The gunner used the elevation wheel and small pulls or taps on the traversing handles to "walk" the gun onto target.

For indirect and overhead fire, individual gun commanders carried out the orders of officers assigned as section or company commanders. In much the same manner as for artillery, these officers received thorough instruction in siting their guns and the mathematics of long distance shooting. Map, compass, clinometer and data tables were every bit as important as the gunner's mechanical skills and the commander's visual acuity.

Water cooling provided the sustained fire capability of the Maxim, allowing, at times, tens of thousands of rounds to be fired almost continuously by multi-gun sections. Coupled with its highly stable and precisely adjustable mount, the MG08's 4,400-yard maximum range was put to most effective use. Aerial photos and detailed maps allowed the combatants to identify enemy positions, support areas, and established avenues of resupply and reinforcement. Using sophisticated mathematics and specially designed aiming equipment, highly trained officers could adjust the "beaten zone" of concentrated machine gun fire directly onto specific enemy strongpoints without needing to observe the strike of the bullets. Gun direction and elevation for several targets could be prepared ahead of time and shoots carried out regardless of darkness, smoke, or foul weather.

Similarly, supporting machine guns could be aimed at high angles over the heads of friendly troops as they charged across No Man's Land. The bullets would plunge downward into the defenders' trenches, disrupting their ability to repel the attackers. This protective fire would be lifted as the lead elements came within a few dozen yards of the objective, and "walked forward" to kill any retreating enemy or reinforcements.

* * *

The ever heavier and more sophisticated artillery, poison gas, and heavy machine guns used by all the combatant powers completely locked the Western Front into vast networks of trenches and underground bunkers from 1915 to 1918.

The deadlock was to some extent broken by the first primitive generation of tanks, but these were only ever an additional factor in the equation - they never changed its nature. Despite the use of all these lethal machineries on an industrial scale, ultimately no advance could be achieved until the "poor bloody infantryman" scrambled out of his ditch and stumbled forward across the nightmare expanse of shell-blasted mud and wire into a maelstrom of flying metal. The machine gun was the king of the last few hundred yards of No Man's Land; and Maxims were the most deadly and efficient of them all, in the hands of British, German, American and Russian gunners.

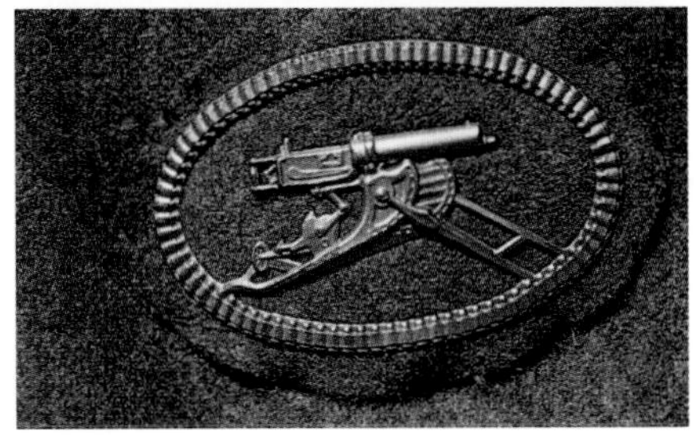

One end of a two-man "stretcher carry" with the MG08 on its sled mount - practical only for relatively short distances, given the weight of 126lbs (57kg). Note the distinctive brass and felt sleeve badge of the "Machine Gun Sharpshooter" - sometimes torn off if capture was imminent, due to the understandable hatred felt by some Allied troops for machine gunners.

BELOW LEFT *In a woodland setting near Rheims, France - well behind the lines - members of a German crew clean their MG08 and repack ammunition boxes. Although generally reliable, the complex MG08 needed regular careful maintainenance and proper adjustment by thoroughly trained crews. (NARA)*

BELOW *France, September 1918: a German sentry wearing the heavy body armour issued to machine gunners, the four torso plates mounted on leather straps and backed with thick felt; note also the extra frontal plate strapped to his helmet, its cut-outs engaging the ventilation horns. (NARA)*

Gunner's eye view of MG08, emplaced with the front legs of the quadripod racked forward horizontally to rest on the low parapet. Note manufacturer's markings and matching serial numbers; on the top cover these are "3392" (serial number)/"d" (inspector's proof mark) /"M.G.08"/ "Gwf.SPANDAU."/ "1917". Serial and inspection mark are repeated on the feed block and at the rear edge of the water jacket.

Upper part of the quadripod showing the sturdy mounting frame for the gun, and the hinged linkage between the frame and the elevating gearbox. Note the leather pad on the rear surface of the front leg; these cushioned the shoulders of the assistant gunner when he carried the mount.

MG08 Technical Specifications

Nomenclature	Maschinengewehr 08
Manufacturer	Deutsche Waffen und Munitionsfabrik (DWM), Gewehrfabrik Spandau
Calibre	7.92mm x 57mm Gewehr Patrone '98
Ammunition	Ball; armour-piercing; tracer
System of operation	Short recoil
Cooling	Water; jacket capacity 7 pints (4 litres)
Selector	None; full automatic only
Feed	250-round cloth belts
Length	44ins (1117mm)
Weight, gun	49lbs (22.2kg) with water, without armour
Weight, mount	77lbs (34.9kg) with accessories
Barrel	28.35ins (720mm); 4 grooves, right twist
Sights	Post front; V-notch rear on leaf; 2.5 power optical scope
Rate of fire	400-500rpm cyclic
Muzzle velocity	2,800fps/(850mps)
Max.effective range	4,400 meters

Lower portion of the sled with controls for the elaborate elevating mechanism; note the locking handle on the left side of the elevation gearbox. Also seen here are boxes and fittings for lubricants, tools, and spare parts; and at far right, one of the comfortable leather kneeling pads on the rear legs.

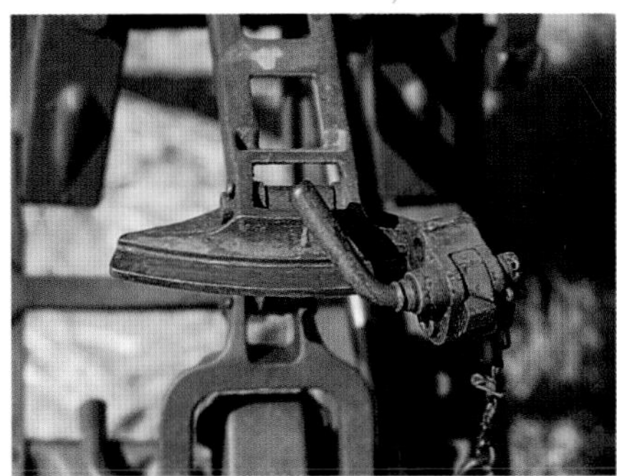

Detail of mounting point at rear of mounting frame, traversing plate, and traverse locking handle. It is puzzling that the designers provided neither a worm gear for left/right movement nor a scale to assist preregistered fire.

LEFT AND BELOW *Placing the gun onto the mount. The front of the gun is supported by trunnions on the top and bottom of the water jacket which fit into sockets in the centres of the mounting frame U-piece and the fold-over top strap, providing pivot points for traversing. The top strap is secured by a wingnut. The water jacket filler is located just to the right rear of the mounting point, and a petcock below the right front end of the jacket was provided for draining.*

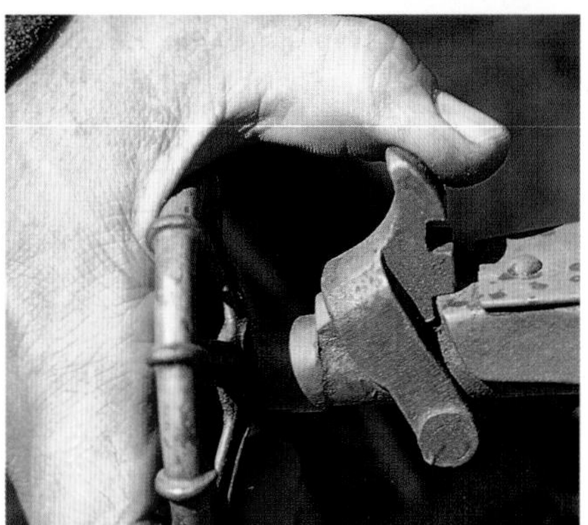

Turning the elevating handwheel clockwise raises the muzzle; its ridges give grip in the wet or cold, and also provide a reference point when making adjustments with the ranging scale on the top of the elevating gearbox. When free movement is needed the gunner thumbs back the locking catch and lifts the handwheel to disengage the elevating gear.

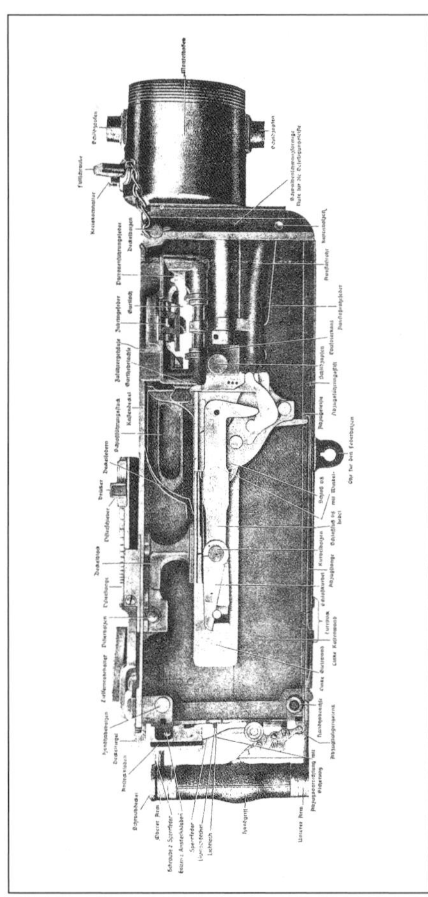

Cutaway of right side of receiver – note the amount of empty space compared to the reduced receiver of the Vickers, p58. From Waffengeschichte Folge, W78, Das Maschinengeweher 08, *Karl Pawlas, Nurenberg. (Author's collection)*

Mechanism

The action of the Maxim MG08 can be likened to a cartridge-powered internal combustion engine. Although functioning on the simple principle of "short recoil", its cycle of operation is a complicated series of movements of parts that require precision manufacture, meticulous adjustment, and near-constant lubrication and cleaning. Indeed, the wartime MG crew course lasted a full month, of which a minority was devoted to actual live fire marksmanship. Most of the student's time was spent learning the care and feeding of the beast, and correcting a daunting catalogue of potential "stoppages".

This thoroughness was commendable; but it also meant that these men were not quickly available to replace mounting casualties. More immediately of concern to tactical leaders was that untrained men were unable to take over critically important guns in the heat of battle when their crews fell. The problem became increasingly acute as the war ground on, compounded by the difficulty of mass manufacture of these marvelously complex guns from increasingly scarce high quality steel, by semi-skilled labour using deteriorating machinery.

Cycle of operation

This book is not intended for the hard-core technical reader; but in this instance the author feels that the complexity of the Maxim system - and by extension, that of a whole generation of machine guns - is best conveyed by quoting the description of the MG08's cycle of operation by the scholar and engineer George M.Chinn in his classic *The Machine Gun*. The action begins with the firing of a chambered cartridge:

"As the powder charge is ignited, pressure builds up and the projectile starts through the bore. During this time the barrel and bolt are securely locked.

"After recoiling ¾ inch, the bolt is unlocked. The crank engages the unlocking cam, breaking the toggle joint and freeing the bolt. The recoiling forces are now able to accelerate the bolt assembly to the rear and rotate the crank. This winds the actuating chain, loading the extension type driving spring (fusee spring) while the recoiling mechanism completes its rearward stroke.

"The initial rotation of the crank pivots the locking lever, forcing the firing pin back against the spring, until the sear engages the sear notch of the lever.

"At the first movement of recoil after unlocking, the sliding (T-slot) boltface begins simultaneous extraction of the empty case from the chamber and withdrawal of a loaded round from the belt. Continued rearward movement engages cams in the receiver to force the sliding boltface downward, bringing the loaded round in alignment with the chamber, and the empty case in position for the ejection tube. The loaded cartridge is held securely in place by a latch arrangement located in the face of the T-slot.

"During recoil a cam lever action moves the entire feed block slide to the right. The top feed pawls move over to engage the incoming round in the belt (being held in position by the bottom belt-holding pawl), at the same time compressing the barrel return spring. After completing its full recoil stroke the forward action of the barrel and barrel extension returns the feed block slide to the left, bringing the next live round in the ammunition belt into position against the cartridge stops for engagement by the sliding T-slot.

"The complete force of recoil having expended itself, the extended driving (fusee) spring starts the movement of counter-recoil. As the bolt moves forward, the cartridge to be fired is positioned for chambering. When this is accomplished, the T-slot rises, 'wipes' itself clear of the spent case and slips over the rim of the incoming round in the belt.

"When the bolt has reached its extreme travel forward, the toggle joint is forced slightly below the horizontal by the connecting rod. At this securely locked position the sear is depressed and disengaged from the firing pin, removing the safety feature, so that continued pressure on the trigger piece permits automatic fire."

Given the intricacy of the action and the number of moving parts it may be imagined that "troubleshooting" the MG08 was an art in itself. The position of the cocking handle when the gun jammed gave a good indication of the probable cause; manuals detail four principal positions, and a host of other eccentricities and pitfalls. Among other possibilities, the gun was prone to stoppages from too much muzzle gland asbestos string packing; shrunken cloth belts; worn or burred lock parts; weak or improperly adjusted springs; and all the usual problems with dirt, moisture, cold, and - specific to the Western Front environment - the corrosive effects of poison gas.

The business end of the MG08 with its distinctive flash cone, flash shield, muzzle booster, and armoured front plate. The off-set post front sight provided a mounting point for this latter, the most widely used of the various armour plates provided. Under the left front of the jacket is the fitting for the steam condenser tube, sealed with a tapered leather plug which pops out if inadvertently left in before firing. It must be removed when attaching a hose - an important bit of "soldier proofing."

An MG08 fitted with bullet- and splinter-proof top and front armour for the jacket, and a top gunner's shield; the port allowed use of both metal and optical sights. This gun is also fitted with a blank-firing device at the muzzle; in action this would be replaced by the arrangement in the top picture. (Courtesy Daniel Murphy).

Thumb pressure on this latch allows the top cover to be lifted, giving easy access to the mechanism.

Removing one of the two spare locks carried in stowage boxes on the sled mount.

The Maxim experience

Our live fire session began on a fine autumn morning at an abandoned coal mine site near Fredericktown, Pennsylvania. After a couple of hours spent in constructing a sandbag emplacement, the noted machine gun manufacturer, gunsmith and enthusiast Charles Erb and I were wishing we had the help of a regulation seven-man German MG08 crew.

Unloading the gun, sled, ammunition, and accessories from the truck and carrying it all a short distance up a small hillside provided further practical explanation for the large size of the crew. . . After several trips and an alarmingly long break to allow heart rates to drop back to fairly normal, we began to assemble the many components of Erb's personal "Grim Reaper" into a functioning engine of war.

The sheer size and complexity of the Maxim and its mount demands some serious mental adjustment by those of us more familiar with the relatively puny and simplified modern "general purpose machine guns." The MG08 is imposingly heavy and *very* big; and faced with all the knobs, scales, compartments, adjustable levers and accessories that seem to stick out at improbable places, one scarcely knows where to begin. Luckily Erb is well versed in the inner and outer workings of his gun and sled system. Starting with the basic operations of emplacing the mount and locking the gun to it, he moved on through water jacket filling, loading, test firing, fusee spring adjustment, sight setting, and use of the traversing and elevating system.

This quickly demonstrated not only that there is a great deal of both Yankee ingenuity and Teutonic logic in the way everything is situated on the gun and mount, but also that a great deal of technical knowledge and specific training is needed for successful operation. Amazingly, it didn't take more than a little tinkering during short burst trial-and-error before Erb had the old gun steadily pumping out bullets at a staid 450 rounds per minute, kicking up great showers of slate trailings from the far side of the mine pit bank.

Firing the MG08

A box is opened and a belt partially withdrawn so that the brass-bound leader tab can be inserted in the feedway. With the cover open to the gunner's inspection, the operating handle is cycled to extract the first round and chamber it with a satisfying "clack". The feed cover is closed and automatically latched in place.

A target is aligned in the 2.5 power optical sight; this is remarkably clear after more than 70 years since its manufacture. Moving the safety lever to one side with slight thumb pressure, the gunner depresses the trigger bar, immediately resulting in a rapid series of explosions. Instantly, the view seen in the scope is obscured by thick dust and flying bits of rock as the 154 - grain bullets, travelling at 2,800fps, impact in the target area. The gun itself has barely moved, and the sharp sound of the report echoes through surrounding hills and dies away.

Another pressure on the trigger bar results in the faintest shuddering vibration of the heavy gun on its massive sled. The canvas belt moves like the sweep second hand of a fine watch, delivering its cartridges to the machine. The arc described by the crank handle is visible to the eye only as a blue-grey smear, as empties squirt out of the ejection tube to rain forward and down. Deflected shock waves from the muzzle booster blast the dirt from sandbags and surrounding

OPPOSITE TOP *The feed block is held in place by the top cover and can be lifted right out of the receiver.*

OPPOSITE BELOW *The fusee spring assembly forces the lock and recoiling parts forward after firing. Its tension must be properly adjusted, by trial and error, to the specific gun, ammunition, and even temperature extremes; this is done using the small sliding lever at the front of the spring housing - note the tension scale on the side of the housing, incrementally marked from 0 to 70.*

ground, raising a fine cloud of dust.

Again and again, long bursts are fired without the hint of a problem. At the end of the 250-round belt the water in the jacket has only slightly heated up, producing a thin wisp of steam from the release valve. I felt completely confident that, given unlimited ammo, water, and spare barrels, this Maxim would just keep on firing for hours on end.

The physical limitations of the range kept us from conducting any accuracy testing beyond 150 meters; but there is ample documentary evidence that the gun is unparalleled in accuracy when fired on point and small group targets out to the extreme edge of optically aided visual observation. In plainer terms, this gun plays aimed Hell well beyond 2,000 meters; and its indirect fire lethality is well proven out to beyond some 4,000 meters - the absolute maximum range of the standard German 7.92mm Mauser service ammunition.

When not using the optics, the metal sights are entirely satisfactory. The leaf rear sight features a sliding bar with a V-notch offset to the left, and is graduated in 50 meter increments out to 2,000 meters. It is not readily adjustable for windage. Although unprotected, the front post is quite sturdy and is offset to the left to match the line of the rear sight. This arrangement is satisfactory under a variety of light conditions.

The cover is removed by pushing up and forward, revealing the heavy fusee spring and its linked attachment to the crank handle on the far side of the receiver. Note the markings on the fusee spring cover.

The sled mount

After cursing the 77lb mount while carrying it into position, I was quickly converted by its rock-steadiness in use. There is no discomfort in pressing your eye right up against the soft leather cup of the optical sight and blasting away. Virtually no recoil is transmitted to spoil your observation of the fall of shot.

Some modern critics have berated its relatively small range of traverse; but, as explained in contemporary manuals, its 30 degrees of left/right movement gives 50 feet of traverse for every 100 yards of distance. This means that a gunner can fire on a line 100 yards wide against advancing enemy troops a mere 200 yards away. Add the fact that several guns were almost always emplaced together on the flanks with interlocking fields of "enfilade" fire; and it seems unlikely that a gunner often needed to grab the rear legs of the mount and yank it to one side to widen the reach of his burst.

The preferred method of loading under combat conditions is with the top cover closed to keep dirt out of the mechanism; here we have left it up for clarity. The gunner pulls a fresh 250-round belt from the ammunition box, inspecting the first several cartridges to ensure that they are still properly seated in the belt after rough handling - improperly seated rounds will cause a failure to feed.

He pushes the brass-bound feed tab into the feed block with one hand and pulls it through with the other until the first cartridge is held tightly against the feed stop. Note the riveted brass spacers on the canvas belt, with an extended spacer in every fifth position (indicating that this is a postwar Belgian belt; original German belts had extensions every three rounds). The extension serves several purposes: it provides a quick visual reference for the assistant gunner that cartridges are properly positioned; keeps belted ammunition in boxes from being jostled out of position by rough handling; and helps guide the belt through the feed block.

Still maintaining pressure on the belt, he rotates the crank handle forward. The lock runs forward and up to slide over the rim of the first round in the belt. Releasing the crank handle allows the lock to pull the cartridge out of the belt. Repeating these motions once again positions the first round for chambering and picks up another from the belt. Close the feed cover, and the gun is ready to fire.

RIGHT *The metal sights are entirely satisfactory for direct fire under all light conditions, using the time-proven V-notch rear and post front off-set to the left of the weapon. The rear sight leaf is marked in 50m increments to 2,000 meters.*

Excellent direct fire aiming results could be attained using the 2.5 power prismatic optical sight. This particularly well preserved model ZF12, manufactured by Emil Busch AG in 1917, was still crystal clear, revealing here an inverted V reticle pattern centred on a "Tommy" silhouette target.

Although the mount can be unlocked for free engagement of targets of opportunity, the MG08 is most efficiently employed using its sophisticated elevating gear and traverse plate. The handwheel extending from the back of the gear box on the mount can be turned to raise or lower the muzzle in precise degrees. This is particularly useful for overhead fire, so that the beaten zone can be "walked" safely in front of advancing troops. The elevation position can be locked using a handle on the left side of the gearbox; free movement can be obtained by releasing a spring catch at the handwheel. A clever scale is provided just forward of the elevating handwheel, usually marked with four curved lines for 800, 1000, 1200, and 1500 meters. When firing at these approximate ranges raising or lowering the beaten zone by 100 meters can be reliably accomplished by turning the handwheel for a rotation distance equalling the length of the line.

Traverse is accomplished with the spade-style handgrips by sliding the gun left or right on its rear mounting plate. Another locking handle, located on the left side of the rear mounting point, allows traverse to be clamped down when needed. Curiously, there is no scale provided on the traversing plate to assist in pre-registering fixed targets.

Several other handy aspects of the MG08 mount include its protected stowage for important spares, tools and two types of lubricant, as well as its ability to be carried alone on one man's back. Two men can carry the mount and gun in stretch-

View of the MG08 firing. Sedately chattering away at 450rpm on its rock-steady mount, it gives little external indication of action save for the dust kicked up in front of the muzzle booster, and the orderly passage of the belt from right to left. Empties are ejected through a tube chute forward and below the receiver. After adjustment of the fusee spring tension the gun began to flawlessly digest a random mixture of odds and ends of 7.92mm ammunition loaded into very old canvas belts. With enough ammunition and water, and barrel changes between each 5,000 to 10,000 rounds, we got the feeling that it would have kept firing without fuss all day long.

er fashion when the front legs are in the fully raised position. Its rounded front allows it to be dragged short distances when under fire, using the heavy slinging straps which were a distinctive part of the machine gun crewman's uniform.

Routine maintenance

As previously stated, the MG08 is a particularly complex internal combustion engine requiring almost constant attention. Many of the duties of the crew revolve around cleaning, oiling, adjusting and protecting the gun from the effects of firing and the ravages of the trench war environment.

A nice bit of "soldier-friendly" engineering is the ability to clean the barrel without removing it from the gun. This saves a lot of trouble in having to drain the cooling jacket, remove the barrel, clean it, then go through the trial-and-error exercise of ensuring that the right amount of asbestos string packing has been wound onto it so that it will recoil freely without letting too much cooling water drip out. After removing the lock and moving the crank handle to its vertical position, a small hole in the backplate can be used to insert a cleaning rod. As any old soldier can tell you, guns should be cleaned from the breech end to avoid burring the muzzle and subsequent loss of accuracy.

This may be an appropriate place to discuss headspace adjustment on the MG08. Simply put, there isn't any. Headspace is the distance between the opening

BELOW *The Maxim gunner's place of work. Top left, the leather eyecup of the ZF12 sight is just visible. Top centre, the metal rear sight leaf is also raised here; note below it the checkered latch for the top cover. The gun's "spade" grips have screw-on top caps, and incorporate oil bottles and brushes. Between them is the checkered oval trigger bar, with the central thumb-slide of the safety catch. Note below this the hole in the centre of the rear plate allowing the barrel to be cleaned without removing it from the jacket.*

Close range firing at a Tommy silhouette to demonstrate the effectiveness of "tapping traverse." When the elevating wheel has been used to get the precise range to the target, the gun is fired while the gunner gives the side of the receiver a series of light taps with his free hand.

to the chamber (breech end of the barrel) and the face of the bolt or lock. It is this distance that determines how much of the base of a chambered cartridge sticks out at the moment of firing. To take into account inevitable variations in the manufacturing tolerances of various component parts from different manufacturers, most heavy machine gun designs provide some way to adjust either the bolt or the barrel to compensate. The Germans decided to go for close manufacturing tolerances and no adjustment. While this did somewhat simplify the mechanism and crew training, it also led to the inevitable nuisance of ruptured cases and separated rims.

Conversely, much hand fitting went into the production of major assemblies for each weapon. That's why key parts such as the feed block and lock assembly of any MG08 are serial-numbered to a specific gun and will not necessarily interchange with others. Imagine the difficulty of crouching in a crowded, dimly lit, smoky bunker while trying to strip, clean, and reassemble your Maxim gun as the concussion of Allied shells causes dirt to rain down on you from the roof. The lock alone has more than 20 parts; then there are the feed block, barrel extension plates, backplate, fusee spring assembly, etc. Even small mistakes could mean a jammed gun in the face of onrushing enemy bayonets.

Functioning is further inhibited by extreme cold when lubricants gum up; the recoiling action of the barrel becomes sluggish, and sometimes even the water in the cooling jacket freezes up. In addition to use of glycerine to retard freezing, an amusing but quite necessary heater box was issued. This clamped onto the water jacket; alas, the heater box could do nothing to thaw and dry a frozen cloth ammunition belt, or the mere humans who were there to pamper and fire it.

Armour

Early battle experience showed that armour protection was necessary for both the gunner and the gun. A single rifle bullet through the water jacket would quickly put the gun out of service, and another through virtually any body part would

ABOVE AND RIGHT *The off-set chamber cleaning tool allows powder residue and other fouling to be removed without stripping the gun; this and several other critical tools are stowed on the sled mount. The oil bottles and brushes fitted inside the spade grips provide instantly available lubrication.*

BELOW *Part of the table of stoppages and the recommended "immediate actions", translated from German manuals and issued to British and American troops for use with captured MG08s. (Author's collection)*

30.—Immediate Action Table—continued.

Position of Crank Handle and its Indication.	Immediate Action.*	Probable Cause.	Prevention of Recurrences.
Third Position: Crank handle almost on check lever.	A.—Lift knob of crank handle, slightly pull belt to left front, give crank handle a glancing blow downward with hand. B.—If "A" fails, examine belt and feed block, if jammed, clear, straighten cartridges in belt, reload, relay and fire. C.—If "B" fails, force down the extractor, change lock, take out first cartridge on belt, reload, relay, and fire.	A.—1. Weak fuzee spring. 2. Friction. 3. Want of oil. 4. Slight fault in feed. B.—1. Bad fault in feed. 2. Bent brass strips. 3. Badly filled belt. 4. Loose pockets in belt. 5. Belt box not in line with FEED BLOCK. C.—1. DAMAGED CARTRIDGE GROOVES. 2. Damaged cartridge rim. 3. Broken gib.	1. Adjust fuzee spring. 2. Test. 3. Re-oil. 4. Keep ammunition box in line with FEED BLOCK or raise the box.
Fourth Position: Crank handle on check lever.	Half load, relay and fire. If gun NOW fails to fire, turn crank handle forward to limit twice and change the lock.	1. Miss-fire. 2. Broken firing pin. 3. Broken lock spring. 4. No cartridge in chamber.	

*If (a), (b) or (c) fail, remove the feed block. Examine the gunmetal valve to ascertain if it is becoming unscrewed. If so, it can be corrected by "hanging" the lock, drawing back the recoiling portions and tapping the gunmetal valve to the *left* with a drift and a hammer.

Some important MG08 accessories (clockwise from top right): The Gurtfuller 16 hand-cranked belt filling machine propped on an ammo box; the water can - note filler cap at one end and turned-in swivel spout at the other, eliminating the need for a separate funnel; the muzzle booster, and the handy "soaking can" in which it could be bathed in solvent to remove carbonisation; Fernglas 08 field glasses; ZF12 optical sight with its leather case; Patronen Kasten 11 double-belt and PK 15 single-belt ammo boxes. (Courtesy Bob Jensen)

immediately do the same for the gunner. Soon four pieces of armour were made available: water jacket front, water jacket top and sides, sled front undershield, sled top gunner's shield. The heavy and awkwardly wide top plate on the gun was abandoned early on, eventually being replaced by a segmented breastplate and helmet plate worn by the gunner and other key crewmen in defensive positions.

Conclusion

The Maxim system represents a milestone not only in the development of military firearms, but in the history of warfare. That it became available in great numbers on the eve of the industrial world's first war of mass national conscription led to an awesome demonstration of its capability: it has even been said that - with the sole exception of the sword - more men have been killed by Hiram Maxim's guns than by any other weapon in history. It is futile to criticise its great weight, or the complexity which required a large and carefully trained specialist crew, from the viewpoint of today's soldier with his light, air-cooled, almost "idiot-proof" general purpose weapons. The Maxim's drawbacks were born - like its extremely impressive strengths - of its own now-distant age of engineering.

Credits

Gun owner & gunner, Charles Erb, Fredricktown, PA; uniform & equipment, George Petersen, National Capitol Historical Sales, Springfield, VA. Primary research sources: Goldsmith, Dolf, The Devil's Paintbrush; Musgrave, Daniel, German Machineguns.

Supposedly an action photo, this is almost certainly a 1917 training shot of an MG08/15 squad at the Sedan battle school - note, e.g., the hurdle flooring in this neat and isolated "shellhole in Flanders". The 08/15 Trupp consisted of a gunner and his assistant plus two ammunition carriers; a second Trupp of seven riflemen and an NCO leader was dedicated to their support in action. (NARA)

MASCHINENGEWEHR 08/15

"The 08/15 light machine gun is only a means whereby the infantry can increase their volume of fire. For mobile defence, the 08/15 is indispensable. It is posted either in the foremost line, or in front of the latter in nests and in shell holes. In the attack, when skillfully handled and judiciously posted, [it] contributes a valuable increase to the volume of fire. It can advance with the first wave of the assault and engage portions of the enemy's trenches where our attack is held up. This demands initiative. Command, as regards both tactical employment and ammunition resupply, should be exercised by the infantry company commander. Only under these conditions can full use be made of this very excellent weapon."
(British Army General Staff/Intelligence translation of a captured German document: quoted Lt.Col.G.S.Hutchison, *Machine Guns*, 1938)

In the first year of the war the heavy machine gun rapidly emerged as the key weapon in defence against massed infantry assaults. But the standard British Vickers Mk1, French Hotchkiss Mle 1914, and German MG08 guns were too heavy, cumbersome and tactically inflexible to be carried forward with any ease in the attack, to suppress defensive fire and to provide support to riflemen against the inevitable counterattack once an objective had been taken.

The solution adopted by the Allies from the mid-war years was to equip their infantry with increasing numbers of Lewis, light Hotchkiss (Benet-Mercié), and Chauchat light machine guns or "automatic rifles". While these weapons were good for their intended purpose, they all suffered from a number of shortcomings (see relevant chapters of this book). Perhaps the most critical of these was absence of a quick-change barrel, leading to severe overheating after firing just a few hundred rounds in a short period of time.

On the German side, it was decided that modifications to the water-cooled MG08 should be undertaken to produce a lighter, more easily managed weapon. The proliferation of small, expedient "trench mounts" in place of the standard sled quadripod bore testimony to the rapidly evolving tactics of trench warfare. Friedrich von Merkatz, a German Army officer and noted authority on machine gun theory and practice, is credited with providing his countrymen with a close support weapon that would not overheat and fail during intense firefights.

Von Merkatz's resulting Maschinengewehr 08/15 (denoting an adaptation of the 08, formally accepted in 1915) used the same internal mechanism, though somewhat modified to lighten the receiver. The MG08's high volume of sustained fire was essentially retained by keeping the water jacket, although reduced in capacity from 4 to 3 liters. A rifle stock, pistol grip, and single trigger were fitted in place of the twin "spade" handles; a simple 1.5lb (.68kg) bipod replaced the massive sled mount; and a hardy tangent rear sight replaced the more delicate leaf. Ready to shoot, with a 100-round belt in a side-mounted Trommel ("drum") belt carrier and a full water jacket, the 08/15 weighed about 43lbs (19.5kg) - only about one-third that of a fully mounted MG08.

Considered from the perspective of the General Staff, the MG08/15 was an excellent adaptation. The same factories could make both guns; many parts and accessories were interchangeable; and soldiers trained on the one could readily operate the other. Fewer men were required for the 08/15's crew, so more guns could be assigned at battalion and even company level as required.

OPPOSITE PAGE *Reconstruction - Westfront, September 1917: an MG08/15 crew from the Bavarian 1.Infanterie-Leib-Regiment von Muenchen (identified by their shoulderstraps and the Unteroffizier's blue/white collar lace) hurry along a communication trench and up "on top" into the wire to bring flanking fire to bear on an Allied attack.*

RIGHT AND OPPOSITE TOP LEFT *The assistant gunner spots and loads for his No.1 in a sandbag-reinforced defensive position. Serving any weapon while wearing World War One gas masks was a trial; the eye pieces fogged up, and they were stuffy and inefficient - particularly this M1917, as the wearer had to breathe both in and out through the filter canister in the absence of an exhalation valve. Note also, on the sandbags, three types of hand grenades: the blast-effect M1915 Stielhandgranate ("stick grenade"); the cast-iron M1916 Eierhand-granate ("egg grenade"); and the M1913 Kuegelhandgranate ("ball grenade"), with a deeply segmented fragmentation casing.*

In the trenches

The picture was rather less rosy from the perspective of the trenches, however. While undeniably more readily transported than the MG08, the 08/15 was still a formidably bulky piece of steel and wood. The water jacket provided excellent cooling; but it was heavy, consumed always-precious drinking water, and had to be protected against freezing during the long, severe winters. Mechanical training was every bit as demanding as for the earlier Maxim, and the clock-like precision of its internal mechanism was equally intolerant of dirt, water, and carbon fouling.

However, it is the soldier's lot to make the best of whatever he is given to work with; and in capable hands the 08/15 - for all its shortcomings - was unde-

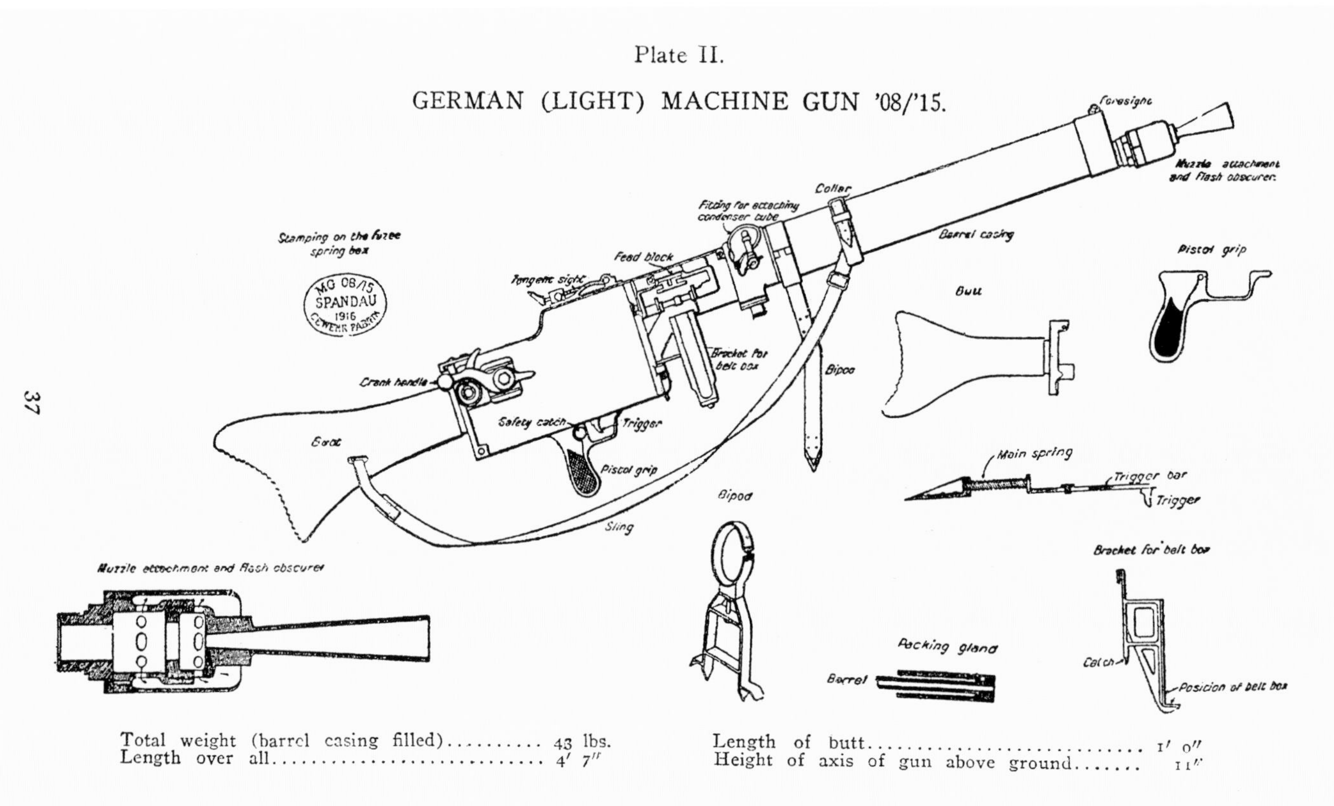

Familiarisation drawing from a wartime British intelligence document (S.S.153), reprinted by the US War Department as Notes on the '08 (Heavy) and '08/15 (Light) German Machine Guns, *Oct.1918. (Author's collection)*

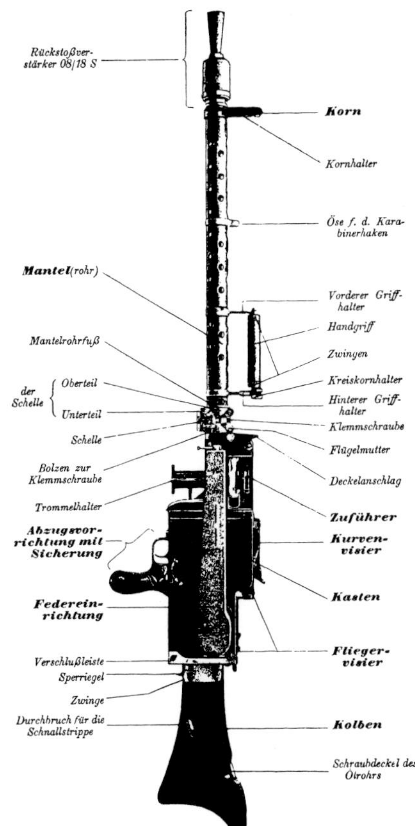

Drawing (from Die Maschinengewehr 08/15 und 08/18*, Berlin, 1935) identifying major components of the MG08/18, the air-cooled version of the wartime MG08/15. It was introduced too late to have any real impact; but postwar developments leading to the superb MG34 would draw heavily on experience with this and other air-cooled designs. (Author's collection)*

niably deadly. By 1916 initial problems were ironed out and production gained speed. As more and more guns reached the front their combined effect began to present serious problems for the Allies.

Throughout 1916 the Germans began to employ light machine guns as an integral asset of each infantry company in key areas of the Western Front, initially at a rate of four per company. The heavy guns were still organised in special detachments within the division and companies within the battalion; but issue of the 08/15 meant that for the first time rifle company commanders had their own machine guns. The immediate tactical value of this was to give front line soldiers direct fire support in both offensive and defensive operations. It was no longer necessary to beg for machine gun fire from battalion or regimental command staff.

If desired, the company commander could place several of his own guns well forward of the main trench line to ensure the best possible defensive application. In the attack, he could count on machine guns firing on the move right alongside his riflemen, and being immediately available to defend newly-won ground against counterattack.

Transformation of the rifle squad

By the end of 1917, German Chief of Staff Ludendorff recognised the clear dominance of the machine gun in the infantryman's arsenal. He carefully analysed the lessons learned in November 1917 at Cambrai, where his forces were initially overwhelmed, but had then counterattacked successfully. In his postwar memoirs he writes of the realisation that machine guns would serve Germany well both in preserving her dwindling manpower, and in eliminating as many of the enemy as possible:

"An important change, moreover, had occurred; the machine gun had to become the chief firing weapon of the infantry. The companies must be provided with new light machine guns, the serving of which must be done by the smallest possible number of men. Our existing machine guns...were too heavy for the purpose."

The standard issue of four light machine guns per infantry company was quickly increased to six. Along with this new development came changes in tactical doctrine which reversed the traditional relationship of the rifleman and the machine gunner in a way which was to have a lasting effect on the character of infantry fighting. Henceforward a machine gun *Trupp* (squad) consisted of one MG08/15, two trained gunners, and two ammunition carriers. They were directly supported by a second *Trupp* made up of a squad leader and seven riflemen. These two elements formed a *Gruppe* (section); and the task of the riflemen was to protect the machine gunners at all costs.

Manoeuvres in the Bavarian Alps, probably early 1930s; note two important postwar improvements to this 08/15 - the bipod has been relocated to the muzzle area for better long range accuracy, and metallic links have replaced the troublesome cloth belts. Note the blank-firing muzzle attachment and the 100-round drum belt carrier. (USACMH)

The belt drum fits onto the bracket fixed on the right of the receiver below the feed block. The fabric belt is prevented from unwinding when not attached to the gun by folding a ratcheted handle against teeth on the outside of the carrier; the stamped and painted warning "Feuer! Kurbelhoch" means "Lift handle before firing" - this disengages the ratchet. Weight fully loaded is 7lbs (3.17kg).

Storm Troops

"Preceded by patrols, the Germans advanced at 7a.m. in small columns bearing many light machine guns and, in some cases, flamethrowers. From overhead low-flying airplanes, in greater numbers than had hitherto been seen, bombed and machine gunned the British defenders, causing further casualties and, especially, distraction at the critical moment. Nevertheless, few posts appear to have been attacked from the front, the assault sweeping in between to envelop them from flanks and rear."

(From the *British Official History of the War*)

At about the same time, the German High Command began to place increasing emphasis on the training and employment of special assault infantry known as *Stosstruppen* (literally "shock troops"), formalised in elite units designated as *Sturmbataillone* - storm or assault battalions. These men were heavily armed with grenades, flamethrowers, and large numbers of light machine guns. Historical accounts show that their automatic weapons of choice were the air-cooled Danish Madsen, captured British Lewis guns, and of course the water-cooled 08/15. (They were also the first to receive the Bergmann MP18 sub-machine gun to further augment their extraordinary firepower - see next chapter.)

The mass frontal attack by whole corps and divisions of infantry, according to inflexible plans which the lack of reliable communications made impossible to adapt to developing events, had proved a murderous waste of men. The most important task of the assault troops - indeed, the reason for their existence - was to spearhead attempts to break through the Allied trench lines by concentrating their mobile firepower on selected sectors isolated by German artillery fire, pressing on to exploit success at their own initiative and leaving the conventional infantry formations that followed to mop up and consolidate. Firepower applied immediately in the service of tactical initiative was the key to their effectiveness, and the MG08/15 was their most available means of delivering that firepower.

The last year of the war saw a tremendous increase in the number of machine guns of all types throughout the German Army. At the same time, addressing the disadvantages of the MG08/15's formidable weight and mechanical complexity, the Germans carried out a number of experiments. Small numbers of the MG08/18 were fielded in the last months of the war; this modification of the 08/15 had a slightly heavier barrel shrouded in a thin, slotted air-cooling jacket, thus eliminating several pounds' weight of steel and water. However, the inherent design of the mechanism would not lend itself to a quick-change barrel, and overheating was inevitably a problem.

The wooden ammunition box holds two sheet metal drums. The fabric 100-round belts were specially made for use with the 08/15.

The crank handle moves forward and backward in an arc during firing. Training manuals feature a table of stoppages with remedial actions to be taken when malfunctions occur, each identified by the position where the crank handle stops.

The top cover markings on this 08/15 are: "6342" (serial number - repeated on the feed block)/ "M.G.08/15"/ "S.& H." (manufacturer Siemens und Halske)/ "BERLIN."/ "1918". Note the canvas sling looping through the leather collar round the barrel jacket; and the filler cap (left) and steam hose fitting (right), located at the rear of the jacket for ease of handling in action.

MG08/15 Technical Specifications

Nomenclature	Maschinengewehr 08/15
Manufacturer	Gewehrfabrik Spandau, DFW, and five lesser firms.
Calibre	7.92mm x 57mm Gewehr Patrone '98
Ammunition	Ball; armour-piercing; tracer; blank
System of operation	Short recoil
Cooling	Water; jacket capacity 5.2 pints (3 litres)
Selector	None; full automatic only
Feed	Cloth belts, 100- and 250-round capacity
Length	55ins (1397mm)
Weight, gun	43lbs (19.5kg) with water & loaded 100-round drum
Barrel	28.25ins (718mm); 4 grooves, right twist
Mount	Bipod & shoulder stock; anti-aircraft tripod
Sights	Post front; V-notch tangent rear
Rate of fire	450-550rpm cyclic
Muzzle velocity	2,800fps (850mps)
Max.effective range	Approx.1,200m

The hose leads back to the water can to condense steam generated by the heat of sustained firing. This special can, used with both the MG08 and the 08/15, has a swivel spout for refilling the jacket.

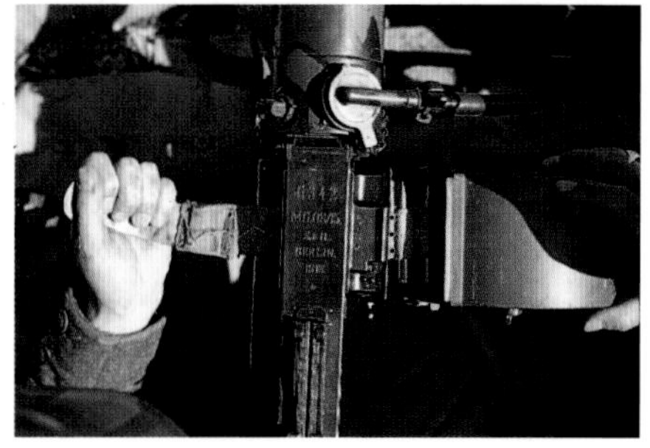

Intolerant of dirt and fouling, the gun should be loaded with the top cover closed. The metal leader tab on the belt (here an original example, with extended brass spacers every three rounds) is passed through the feed block from right to left; tension is maintained on the belt as the crank handle is cycled forward and backward twice, allowing the lock to withdraw a cartridge from the belt and seat it into the chamber.

The sturdy tangent rear sight is adjustable in 100m increments out to an improbable 2,000m. The open V-notch gives good accuracy in all light conditions.

The high quality of the 08/15 manual is indicated by this meticulous illustration showing the correct procedure for lubricating the lock. (Author's collection)

Firing the MG08/15

Our photo session took place in late September in the trench network maintained by the Great War Association near Shimpstown, Pennsylvania. Richard Keller, a WWI historian, collector, militaria dealer and re-enactor, served as the gunner with his personal MG08/15; Denny Wingert served as assistant gunner.

Like its heavier parent, the so-called "light Maxim" is an impressive and formidable piece. Precision crafted from hardwood and machined steel, the 43lb 08/15 is unforgiving to all but the strongest and best-trained gunners. There are good reasons why German "Machine Gun Sharpshooters" were hand-picked from among volunteers and given several weeks of intense mechanical and live fire training.

After an hour or so of static photography of the gun, its accessories and operations, the time came to actually shoot it. We started with a dry water jacket in order to evaluate the difference in handling and accuracy between an empty gun and one filled with cooling water.

Keller lifted the feed cover and threaded the leader of a 100-round belt into the feed block. As he rotated the crank handle forward and back twice, we watched the smooth movements of the beautifully machined lock system as it withdrew a cartridge from the belt and delivered it to the chamber. The gunner lowered the feed cover and snapped it shut with a firm tap of the fist. Pushing off the safety, he took a breath and squeezed the trigger. The gun came to life - briefly; as the echoes died away over the Pennsylvania countryside we gazed, in the silence, at the motionless crank handle.

Immediate action

We compared the position in which the handle had stopped with the diagram in the gunner's manual showing common malfunctions and their cure. Deciding that it was a "third position stoppage" (crank handle almost touching the crank lever), Keller placed the gun on SAFE and performed the first "immediate action" step specified: lifting the knob of the crank handle, pulling the belt out and forward, then tapping the crank handle back down toward the crank lever.

A second burst was also cut short, leaving the crank once again in the "third position." Deciding that the most probable cause among the listed options was a weak fusee spring, Keller gave a few turns to the adjustment lever on the left side of the gun, increasing tension on the spring to fully return the lockface to the front of the receiver. The third burst vindicated this choice, as a satisfying string of about 25 rounds ripped downrange.

With the gun functioning smoothly, Keller gave me a chance to get behind it and squeeze off a few bursts myself. I dropped to a prone position and raised the buttstock to my shoulder, noticing how its deeply scooped contour helped to keep the gun in place. While the starkly vertical pistol grip is rather awkwardly placed quite low under the receiver, it is a robust fistful. The trigger guard is big enough to allow easy access for a thickly gloved finger, and the safety is well positioned and easily operated by thumb pressure of the firing hand. By some Germanic logic that eludes me, it is easier to put on SAFE (pushed forward) than on FIRE. A helpfully large pictograph on the left side of the receiver reminds absent-minded gunners of the relative positions.

The sights

The rear sight is positioned at a neck-stretching height above the receiver, but at least it is of the handy tangent design. The traditional German V-notch rear and post front configuration is used, making for quick target engagement even under low light conditions. Adjustments in range - in 100m increments between 400m and 2,000m - are quickly and easily made by squeezing in the spring plunger at the sight base and sliding it into position. No provision is made for anyone but the unit armourer to make adjustment of windage, but natural dispersion of the burst tends to compensate adequately.

The mount

There has been much criticism of the 08/15's chunky little bipod, but it is not easy to suggest what to do about it. Placed rather forward of the gun's approximate centre of gravity, it allows fast and wide traverse, but too much rocking when firing. While placing it at the muzzle end would have greatly improved accuracy, it would also have put most of the gun's considerable weight back on the gunner, with resulting fatigue. Dolf Goldsmith, in his encyclopaedic *The Devil's Paintbrush*, suggests that a small, rudimentary tripod would have been a better choice; but would the weight penalty and knee-banging awkwardness have been acceptable?

Prone firing, "dry" and "wet"

I lined up the sights on a suitable target among the sandbags of the opposing trench complex some 200 meters away, and tightened up on the trigger. The heavy,

Prone firing. The 08/15 showed to its best advantage when fired supported. Gently rocking with each burst, the "light Maxim" runs through belt after belt with clockwork precision. With so little actual recoil and such a long barrel, one would expect exceptional accuracy. However, given the poor positioning of the bipod and the water sloshing around in the jacket, practice and muscle are needed to keep it on target beyond 600 meters; and we gave way to the temptation to remove the bipod and rest the jacket on sandbags. Note **TOP LEFT** *the crank handle in mid-cycle, and an ejected empty silhouetted against the sling below the receiver. As with the MG08, dust kicked up by muzzle blast is the only other sign that this gun is firing fully automatic.*

sturdy gun shuddered with recoil and tapped my shoulder lighty but firmly. The burst flew over the intended impact area and kicked up a satisfying amount of dust a bit higher on the hillside. Since the sights are adjustable only in 100m increments, it was necessary to use "Kentucky windage" and re-aim rather lower than the centre of the target. My second burst was easily "walked" right up into the mound of sandbags.

After waiting a few minutes for the barrel to cool a bit, we then filled the water jacket from the handy little can invented by the Germans early in the war. The big, round prewar cans were soon abandoned in favour of one the same size and shape as the 1915 pattern 250-round ammo can with its characteristic offset handle; this allowed easy stowage and transport, and its built-in swivel spout eliminated the need to keep separate funnels in the trenches. However, the small apertures of the jacket and spout make for slow filling and require a steady hand. One "soldier friendly" point is the relocation of the steam exit hose to the rear of the water jacket; this allows the gunner or assistant to perform all water-related operations without crawling forward or pulling the gun back from its prepared position.

Detail of the 08/15's complex lock (bolt), arranged to show the three positions of cartridges during the firing cycle, left to right: (1) Cartridge is extracted from belt. (2) It slides down face of lock after it is chambered, as lock rises to engage another cartridge in feed block. When lock has fully risen, firing pin is released to detonate chambered cartridge. Recoil action drives mechanism rearward, simultaneously extracting fired cartridge and drawing new cartridge from feed belt. (3) Fusee spring pulls lock mechanism forward again to eject fired case, chamber the middle one, and grasp the top one.

The drawing (top) from Das Maschinengewehr *08/15 by Maj.Friedrich von Merkatz, published in Berlin in 1918, shows the safe method for clearing a stoppage when the gun is loaded: the lock must be firmly grasped so that the centre cartridge cannot be inadvertently fired. (Author's collection)*

After filling up the jacket with the requisite 5¼ pints the "wet test" proceeded. Conventional wisdom holds that a heavier gun is a more accurate gun, and this is true up to a point - the point when the water begins to slosh around inside the jacket. Keller had spoken knowingly of this phenomenon but I had foolishly discounted the realities of fluid dynamics. The mid-mounted bipod and the "wave" effect really work their mischief on the 08/15. Where previously there was only recoil impulse to contend with, now the natural rocking action of the gun on firing was augmented by this wave action; it shouldn't be overstated, but the two separate, simultaneous rhythms are quite disconcerting while trying to keep the sights on target. As one can well imagine, the effect gets even more pronounced at longer ranges. Better luck was experienced by resting the jacket on a handy sandbag.

Assault firing

Assault fire on the move is another formidable feat with the 08/15. At twice the weight of an American M60 machine gun with bipod the German gun is a front-heavy handful. Even suspended from its wide sling it was uncomfortably heavy and unbalanced. Gunners had to be chosen from the largest, strongest men available, and even they could not hope to advance at more than a fast walk with 43lbs of dead weight around their necks. I'm told that the big, heavy Trommel was not often used in the trenches, and that its short 100-round belts were not nearly as popular as the standard 250-round version; but I am tempted to challenge this by imagining what it must have been like having to drag 10 to 15 feet of expended belt through the mud and wire of No Man's Land.

However, the photos we took of Keller blasting away from the hip at cardboard "Tommies" show that assault fire can be delivered effectively - and, after all, this is the near-miracle that von Merkatz was able to wring out of the Maxim gun. The hardest trick seems to be just getting the beast up the ladder and over the parapet of your own trench in the first place.

In prone and hip firing we were able to put over 500 rounds through the gun with only an occasional stoppage, all of which were easily cleared. The water cooling system lived up to expectations, the jacket getting only slightly warm to the touch. We didn't have the ammo necessary to get up a full boil with the resulting plumes of position-disclosing steam; and thankfully, we didn't experience scalded fingers from escaping steam while trying to steady the spout and refill the jacket as the enemy rushed us with fixed bayonets. With no one shooting back at us, no artillery showering us with hot steel and dirt, no mud in the action or ice on the belts, we could have continued to fire as long as the ammunition held out. For the German soldier of the Great War things were not so easy. The 08/15 requires a lot of care and adjustment from a thoroughly knowledgeable gunner to keep it reliable when the going gets tough. There are ample reasons why captured Lewis guns were so highly prized.

Although very heavy, the 08/15 can be carried by one man on the broad sling provided. The bipod could be carried as shown, hung over the gunner's or assistant's bayonet hilt.

As soon as the Allied barrage lifts the MG crews come streaming out of their bunkers to repulse the inevitable infantry assault. They work their way to assigned positions along the trench lines before throwing the gun up on the sandbagged parapet. Note how the gunner has to grasp the trailing expended end of the ammunition belt to keep from tripping over it or snagging it in the wire.

Assault firing. Our gunner described crawling under a barbed wire entanglement with the 43lb (19.5kg) 08/15 as "like dragging an engine block". Going "over the top" with this awkward weight slung for assault fire is a job only for the strongest men. Moving assault fire is possible, but not easy, due both to the weight and the poor balance of the gun; note the awkward appearance of the gunner's right hand grasping the pistol grip below the deep receiver.

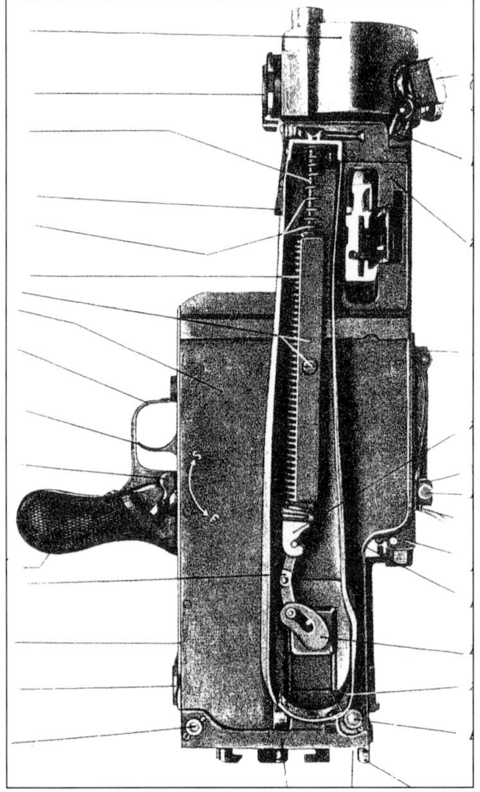

The fusee spring mechanism is revealed in this left side view from the manual, with cover removed. Note also, above the pistol grip, the safety lever with "S-Sicher" and "F-Feuer" positions marked above. (Author's collection)

Conclusion

The MG 08/15 represented a largely successful stage in the evolution from first generation heavy machine guns to the lighter and more portable dual-purpose guns which would appear during the years between the wars. Heavy, awkward, and requiring a high degree of mechanical aptitude and care, the 08/15 nonetheless provided the German Army with decisive firepower in both defensive and offensive situations, and heralded the significant transformation of small unit tactics. A staggering 130,000 were manufactured by seven firms in less than 24 months during the war.

Credits

Gun owner & gunner, uniforms & equipment, Richard Keller, Great War Militaria, Chambersburg, PA; assistant gunner, Denny Wingert, Chambersburg, PA; location assistant, John Exley IV, Mechanicsville, VA; range, Great War Association, Shimpstown, PA. Primary research sources: Goldsmith, Dolf, *The Devil's Paintbrush*; Musgrave, Daniel, *German Machineguns*.

STRIPPING THE MG08/15

More or less the identical sequence applies equally to the MG08; in both cases it begins with applying the safety and draining the water jacket.

Slide the fusee spring cover up and forward to open it, then disconnect the spring from its links.

Depress the feed cover latch and lift the cover. If a belt is in place, depress the tab at the rear of the opening to the feed block and withdraw the belt. Cycle the crank handle to extract and eject the chambered round.

Lift the feed block up and out of the receiver.

ABOVE LEFT *To remove the lock, rotate the crank handle forward while lifting the lock straight up and out of the receiver.*

ABOVE *Twisting the lock one-quarter turn either way disengages the interrupted threads. Although identical in design to that of the MG08 it is slightly smaller and not interchangeable.*

Withdraw the fastening pin, then lift up the end plate latch to allow the buttstock group to be rotated down and out of the way.

Withdraw the side plates, barrel extension, and barrel as a group through the rear of the receiver.

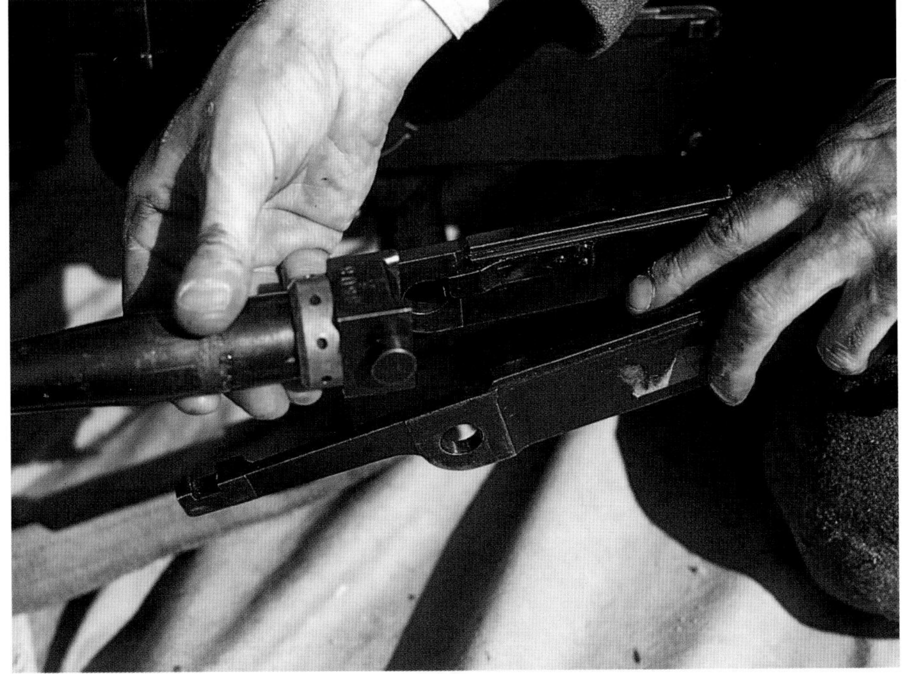

Separate the barrel extension from the side plates. The grey line between the right thumb and forefinger is asbestos string packing forming a gasket to keep cooling water from leaking out of the water jacket. Often mistaken for a headspace adjustment, the tapered brass collar threaded on the barrel is a buffer for the recoiling parts as they run forward under fusee spring tension; a round-nosed pry tool is inserted into the holes to rotate the collar for adjustment.

Detail of the Ruckstossverstarker (muzzle booster/flash suppressor) of the Maxim system, which traps a portion of the propellant gas from each shot to boost rearward thrust of the barrel. This important component produces a 40-50 per cent increase in the cyclic rate of fire, and more positive function in dirty or cold guns.

***Field strip layout with accessories (top to bottom, left to right):** Ammo box; MG08/15; water can; barrel with extension and side plates; recoil booster/flash hider; belt carrier; feed block; lock; fusee spring cover. The gunner's equipment includes Fernglas 08 field glasses, stick grenade, canteen and bread bag, Pistole 08 (Luger), 1917 model gas mask and canister, and 1917 model Stahlhelm.*

Sedan, France, May 1917: two assault infantrymen of the Stosstruppen pose in typically reduced field equipment. Note the sandbags tied together and hung around the neck for stick grenades; the short Kar98a rifles carried slung; the long handled wire cutters, and two canteens, carried by the soldier on the right. (NARA)

MASCHINENPISTOLE 18/I

"We found that the advancing Germans had infiltrated between our gun posts and we came under a hot machine gun fire at close range. Why we were not immediately torn to ribbons passes my comprehension. We dropped to the ground... and while machine gun bullets flicked past our ears and ripped the haversacks on our backs, we worked our way down the furrows... clawing at the earth as we travelled on our stomachs. With the commander of Company A, I stormed the windmill which had fallen into German hands, and we recaptured it in a hand-to-hand fight with the German Storm-Troops." (Narrative of the Battle of the Lys, 12-18 April 1918, quoted Lt.Col.G.S.Hutchison, *Machine Guns*, 1938)

The Bergmann MP18 was the first true sub-machine gun to be widely used in wartime. Introduced in the waning months of WWI as a handy and deadly tool for trench-clearing by elite German assault units, its usefulness inspired postwar development of the world famous Thompson sub-machine gun and the countless other designs which have followed up to the present day.

Its identification as the first sub-machine gun is sometimes challenged by champions of the bizarre little 16lb Italian Villar Perosa twin light machine gun, created by Abiel Revelli and used by Italian Alpine troops as early as 1915. However, despite using pistol calibre ammunition the Villar Perosa was neither suitable nor tactically employed as a hand-held short range assault and defensive weapon; and although examples captured at Caporetto in October 1917 were no doubt studied with interest, the known timing of Hugo Schmeisser's design work at the Bergmann factory makes it incredible that this very different weapon played any real part in the genesis of the sub-machine gun. The honours must clearly go to Schmeisser's Maschinenpistole 18, which pioneered operational principles and physical characteristics still found in modern sub-machine guns some 80 years later. Born as a direct response to the new tactical environment of the Great War trenches, this gun is a landmark in the history of small arms.

Weapons do not spring to life of their own accord in anticipation of some possible future use; like any other tool devised by mankind, to a great extent they are products of necessity.

By 1916 the war in Europe had long been confined to more or less static trench lines. Infantry soldiers were repeatedly forced to conduct suicidal human wave attacks across an increasingly impassable killing zone separating the two lines of field fortifications which stretched hundreds of miles from the North Sea to Switzerland. Two major tactical theories were tested in attempts to break the deadlock. One was the French idea of "walking fire", whereby advancing troops would shoot on the move to keep the defenders' heads down. This quickly proved to be disastrous, because their existing automatic rifles were inadequate and German long range supporting artillery and machine gun fire was so horribly effective.

The training school at Beuville near Sedan, founded by Willi Roehr's 5th Army cadre unit, was the first established for instructing infantry in storm troop tactics. Here assault infantry on a realistic training exercise advance through a barbed wire entanglement, with rifles slung to leave hands free for grenades (far left) and wire cutters (far right). Gen.Ludendorff's recognition that the grenade was virtually replacing the rifle as the trench fighter's weapon of choice - as it also was among British troops - played a part in expediting the development of the MP18. (NARA)

Storm troops

As mentioned in the previous chapter, the other concept was to precede the massed frontal assault with tightly focused thrusts by self-reliant units of unusually heavily armed assault troops. Moving as fast as local circumstances allowed, and exploiting the initiative to isolate and bypass pockets of resistance, these "storm troops" were to penetrate as deeply as possible - ideally, as far as the enemy artillery lines - while conventional infantry mopped up behind them. Credited

Reconstruction - Westfront, October 1918: An Unteroffizier of Bavarian Sturmtruppen from the 1.Jaeger-Bataillon "Prinz Ludwig" advances into action armed with an MP18/I. He wears the M1916 helmet with segment-painted camouflage, and the oiled leather M1917 gas mask; his old M1910 field grey tunic bears late war rank braid on the collar, and a black cut-out stick grenade sleeve badge.

The warrior mystique of the storm troops was promoted to capture the imagination of the increasingly exhausted "home front". Artist Fritz Erler produced this famous image of an idealised young assault trooper for a war loan poster: "Help Us Win." Note the stick grenades carried in sandbags, their safety caps removed and the fuze pull-beads hanging free. (War Memorial Museum, Newport News, VA)

ABOVE RIGHT *The 9mm Parabellum model 1914 Lange-Pistole 08 with clip-on shoulder stock and 32-round "snail" drum magazine extension - the famous "artillery Luger" used by some German trench raiders before the appearance of the MP18. Below is a standard 9mm Pistole 08, the archetypal Luger, which remained virtually unchanged from 1908 until German production ceased in 1942.*

Photographs from a German instruction manual show the special canvas and leather carriers for the "snail" drum magazines used with the long-barrelled "artillery Luger"; when available, they were presumably also used by men armed with the MP18/I. Below is a view inside the sturdy metal Patronen-Kasten for five drums and a magazine filler tool. (Courtesy Don Thomas, Marietta, GA)

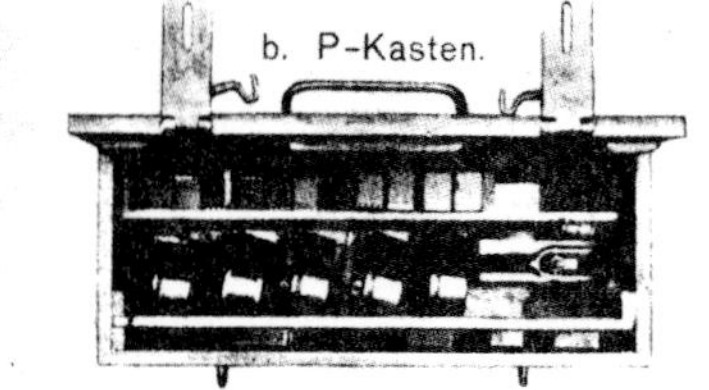

to the German Gen.von Hutier on the Eastern Front in September 1917, these infiltration tactics were in fact discussed in print in 1915 by the French Capt.Laffargue; but it was the German Army which perfected and exploited them, particularly in the great "Michael Offensive" of spring 1918. The storm troops had their genesis in a special combat engineer/artillery assault unit - Sturmabteilung Calsow - formed in May 1915; this came under command of Hauptmann (Captain) Willi Roehr on 8 August 1915. Organizing his new unit into numerous closely co-ordinated small groups armed with a higher than usual proportion of hand grenades and machine guns and supported by light field guns, trench mortars and flamethrowers, he drilled them to advance in a series of short sprints from one shell hole to another, taking advantage of the terrain for cover and concealment, working closely with supporting artillery. An important psychological factor was provided by Roehr's collaborator Maj.Hermann Reddemann, CO of the flamethrowers of the 3rd Guard Pioneers; it was Reddemann who was credited with naming Roehr's assault groups *Stosstruppen* or shock troops.

That autumn Roehr's unit was designated as the training cadre for new assault companies in each division of the 5th Army. In time each division would have a *Sturmkompanie* and each Army a *Sturmbataillon*; and some 17 battalions had been formed by early 1917. The far-sighted Gen.Erich Ludendorff, Chief of the German General Staff from August 1916, knew that Germany could not hope to match the Allies man for man and shell for shell; she had to implement economy of force in both offensive and defensive doctrine, making the best use of available manpower, and Ludendorff was determined to disseminate the new shock tactics throughout his armies.

Crawling out under cover of darkness, gas and smoke, armed with grenades, knives and pistols, the early shock groups would infiltrate between enemy strong-points to cut telephone lines and barbed wire. Having deprived their foe of the ability to report activity and call in supporting artillery, they would then assist the main attack by conventional infantry formations by showering enemy machine gun positions and command bunkers with hand grenades and close range fire. Mobile machine gun teams armed with the MG08/15, Madsen M1914 and captured Lewis guns provided close fire support.

While this concept proved to be very productive, shock troop leaders are reported to have asked their superiors for a new type of machine gun capable of being carried easily by one man. They needed something hardy, simple, reliable, and capable of efficient killing at short to medium range.

Development

As luck would have it, development was already underway in the Theodor Bergmann small arms works at Suhl, then under the direction of one Hugo Schmeisser. Beginning in 1916, Schmeisser had been working to adapt the blow-back-operated Bergmann semi-automatic pistol into a workable automatic weapon. The tactical value of such a weapon had been proved in the trenches by soldiers carrying adaptations of standard military service pistols. Some Pistole 08 (Luger) and M1896 Mauser "Broomhandle" semi-automatics were fitted with shoulder stocks, lengthened barrels, extended capacity magazines and, in a few reported cases, selective fire capability. Although these beautifully machined weapons were extremely succeptible to jamming from battlefield dirt, when they did work they could be quite undeniably deadly. It is reported that the long-barrelled so-called "artillery model Luger" with a 32 round "snail" drum magazine could be emptied in less than ten seconds of semi-auto fire - i.e. even when fired by 32 separate pulls on the trigger.

The exceptional simplicity of the mechanism is readily apparent from this artist's cutaway of the MP18/I. The bolt is held to the rear by a pivoting sear. When the trigger is squeezed the bolt is released to run forward under pressure from the compressed recoil spring, stripping the waiting cartridge from the magazine and driving it into the chamber, where it will be fired an instant before the bolt slams home. (© 1997 G.P.Schurman, reproduced by permission)

In pursuit of the logical but challenging next step - to produce a simple, rugged and portable machine pistol capable of automatic fire while remaining controllable and resistant to jamming - Schmeisser chose to retain the blowback system of operation as being the simplest and most reliable, and then enclosed it in a tubular receiver to protect it against dirt. The extremely high rate of fire of converted pistols was undesirable: it was inaccurate, a waste of ammo, and very hard on the mechanism - all natural consequences of operating a light bolt with a relatively powerful cartridge. To get around this without fitting his gun with an enormously heavy bolt, Schmeisser adapted the technique of advanced primer ignition (API).

The theory of API is to fire the primer an instant before the bolt is fully forward, but not before the cartridge is fully chambered. The bolt, riding forward under pressure of the driving spring, is still in forward motion at the instant of detonation. This forward motion of the bolt must first be overcome before the backward recoil force of the detonating cartridge can stop the bolt and drive it to the rear again; and this opposition of forces absorbs much of the recoil. This ingenious solution allows a moderate cyclic rate without complicated rate reducers or doubling the bolt mass.

As well as can be determined, a successful prototype gun was tested and accepted by the Army late in 1917. First production models were officially designated Maschinenpistole 18; it is ironic that this weapon designed by Hugo Schmeisser has always been popularly called the "Bergmann", while the famous WWII Erma MP38 series, designed by Heinrich Vollmer, is commonly misnamed the "Schmeisser".

The Bergmann MP18 is remarkable for the number of design characteristics which remain more or less standard even in today's sub-machine guns. It is relatively simple to make with standard machine tools, requiring modest tolerances, basic machinist skills, and no special materials other than small arms specification steel. The hardy receiver and barrel jacket are made from heavy gauge steel tubing, and the thick hardwood stock is exceptionally strong. Well able to stand up to inevitable battlefield abuse, it could also be used in hand-to-hand emergencies as a sturdy club (though the failure to provide a bayonet lug is puzzling).

The theoretical or cyclic rate of fire was approximately 400 rounds per minute, and it took standard German 9mm Parabellum pistol cartridges. The widely available 32-round Luger "snail" drum magazine was pressed into service. Because the operating parts were shielded inside the receiver the MP18 was much less susceptible to stoppages than pistols. Firing from an "open bolt" (i.e. the firing cycle begins and ends with the bolt positioned at the rear of the receiver) allowed efficient cooling and eliminated the danger of "cook-off" (when a chambered round is accidentally detonated by excessive heat build-up in the chamber from rapid fire). Finally, its inherent simplicity and heavy weight make it easy to maintain and to shoot with little specialised training and practice.

Minor modifications were applied after a short period of service, and full production was implemented as the MP18/I (in contemporary sources written as MP18,I). The German High Command were apparently so favourably impressed by either the anticipated or actual utility of the gun that the official deployment plan called for arming every officer and NCO and one out of every ten enlisted men in line infantry companies with the new machine pistols. A special machine pistol detachment was also to have been created in each company, consisting of six MP18 gunners, six ammunition carriers - and three ammunition handcarts! We may speculate from this that tactical doctrine anticipated enormous expenditure of ammunition, on a scale roughly equivalent to that of heavy Maxim MG08 sections.

US Army Ordnance Corps photo of a Danish Madsen M1916 light machine gun captured from German troops in France; note the large cone-shaped flash hider and the somewhat impractical provision for a bayonet. This excellent air-cooled automatic weapon in 8mm Mauser rifle calibre was used in large numbers by German assault units, its relative portability and firepower pointing the way to development of a light, pistol calibre "trench sweeper". (NARA)

Light equipment for a local raid or patrol carried by our Bavarian storm trooper. He has a spare magazine for his MP18/I "bullet-squirter" tucked in his belt; the rifle ammunition pouches on his belt are retained, often being used for carrying tobacco, chocolate, etc. as well as packeted 9mm rounds. The gas mask is carried round the neck for instant use; its canister, together with the issue breadbag, canteen and entrenching tool, are slung behind.

The "Kugelspritz"

The storm troops must have embraced their new weapon with fervour; and their nickname for it was *Kugelspritz* - "bullet squirter". It was in front line use for approximately six months before the war ended on 11 November 1918. Although some 35,000 guns are reported to have been manufactured, there is little to be found in historical accounts as to their actual effectiveness in combat. However, it takes little imagination to appreciate the effect that even a handful of men so armed must have been able to produce on a trench full of Allied troops. Following the blast of their customary hail of grenades, Germans with blazing machine pistols would leap into key positions such as machine gun and artillery emplacements and command dug-outs, sawing down the defenders before they could bring their long, clumsy rifles to bear.

The battlefield effectiveness of this new weapon was certainly not overlooked by the Allies, since their Disarmament Commission later ruled that the 100,000-man postwar German Army was not allowed to keep the MP18. Large numbers were destroyed, and the balance were given to the Weimar Republic's "Green Police" for internal security use. (These latter guns are readily identified by a 1920 re-stamp on the magazine housing.) Many of the MP 18/I and 1920 re-stamped guns were further modified by Schmeisser - now employed by C.G.Haenel - to take straight, box-type magazines of 20 or 32 rounds. Subsequent evolutionary machine pistol designs building directly on Schmeisser's work were the MP28/II from Haenel and MP34/I from Bergmann.

The M1915 Stielhandgranate was issued in large numbers to the storm troops, and a cloth silhouette of a grenade was sewn to the sleeve as a badge of their status by some such units. The cylindrical metal head came with a flat belt hook attached. These 1916-18 production examples have a tin screw cap at the end of the handle, protecting the pull bead and cord of the 5½ second friction fuze; note fuze delay reminder stamped on the handle.

MP18/I Technical Specifications

Nomenclature	Maschinenpistole 18,I
Manufacturer	Theodor Bergmann Abt Waffenbau, Suhl
Calibre	9mm x 18mm Pistole Patrone 08 (9mm Luger/Parabellum)
Ammunition	Ball
System of operation	Blowback with advanced primer ignition
Cooling	Air
Selector	None; full automatic only
Feed	32-round "snail" drum magazine
Length	32.10ins (815mm) overall
Barrel	7.88ins (200mm); 6 grooves, right twist
Weight w/out mag.	9.25lbs (4.26kg)
Weight,mag.loaded	11.6lbs (5.33kg)
Sights	Post front, two-position V-notch rear (100m & 200m)
Rate of fire	400rpm
Muzzle velocity	1,362fps (415mps)
Max.effective range	200-300 meters

LOADING THE "SNAIL" MAGAZINE

Before loading the magazine spring must be wound to the proper tension with the attached lever, which is then secured in a handy keyhole notch. Loading begins by depressing the lever of the special loading tool and inserting cartridges one at a time; the lever is allowed to ride upward under spring pressure, and another round is put into position for a downward stroke. The magazine held 32 rounds, but short loading to a maximum of 28 is recommended.

A special sheet metal collar on the straight section extending from the snail drum provides a necessary reinforcement and spacer designed to help steady the Luger magazine when it is used with the MP18/I. In his left hand our gunner holds the sheet metal cover that protects the feedway of the magazine from dirt and damage when outside the gun.

The only safety catch is the slot marked "S" (Sicher - Safe) into which the bolt cocking handle can be rotated by pulling it right back; it can jerk out if the gun is dropped, leading to accidental discharge if loaded. The gun can be loaded with the bolt forward or back, but the latter is best. Insert the magazine into the sharply angled housing until it clicks into place. The angle of the magazine feedway is necessary to position cartridges in line with the axis of the bolt and chamber.

The large knurled magazine release button is well placed and easily operated by the left thumb. Note also the markings on the receiver: "M.P.18,I."/(Bergmann factory proof mark)/"2381" (serial number).

Firing the MP18/I

The first step in preparing the gun for firing is loading the magazines; the accompanying photos show the relatively complicated sequence required to fill the unusual 32-round "snail" drums. Never designed from first principles as the ideal magazine for this or any other weapon, but rather as an ingenious stop-gap modification to the existing Luger pistol magazine, its awkwardness is not surprising. These expensive magazines suffered from numerous problems, e.g. broken mainsprings, malfunctions through dirt and dents, and lost loading tools. The conventional box magazines introduced after the war were a more practical solution.

Perhaps the most obvious drawback of the MP18 is its poor balance as a result of this large drum magazine. Jutting out sideways for almost a foot, and weighing 2.35lbs (1.06kg), it is a definite liability when trying to deliver aimed fire from a standing position. However, when firing from the hip or prone supported positions the magazine housing provides an excellent grip, and balance is acceptable.

Shooting the MP18 is substantially unlike any other sub-machine gun in my relatively wide experience. The first thing the shooter notices on picking it up is its sheer weight - at 11.6lbs (5.33kg) it is heavier than a standard German Gew98 infantry rifle and bayonet, making it a significant load to carry for any length of time, and requiring a noticeable effort to bring it up to the shoulder for standing aimed fire. On the other hand, this mass absorbs all of the recoil of its 9mm Parabellum cartridges and the cycling of the bolt is hardly noticed, making for an exceptionally stable "firing platform".

The magazine is positively locked in the housing by its magazine catch, allowing little free play. A large, sturdy, gently curved bolt-retracting handle sticks out on the right side of the receiver, providing a man-sized surface to grab and operate. Rudimentary safety is attained by rotating this cocking handle up into a slot in the receiver. This is not 100 per cent reliable, as there is still no positive means to keep the bolt from being bounced out of the slot and running forward to fire the gun if the MP18 is accidentally dropped on its butt.

The conventional shape of the buttstock was probably chosen in deference to tradition and because this enabled any ordinary rifleman to pick up and effectively fire the gun without transitional training. For the same reason the sights are the time-honoured German standard V-notch rear and post front. The rear sight is adjustable only for 100m and 200m by flipping the L-type hinge. No windage adjustment is provided. The trigger is located inside a rather large and substantial guard allowing a gloved finger easy access. The large knurled magazine catch affords easy operation without being overly susceptible to accidental release.

Cycle of operation

Starting with a loaded magazine in place, the bolt is drawn back by pulling the cocking handle until the sear engages. When the trigger is pulled this tips forward to push the sear rod, in turn rotating the sear downward from its notch in the bottom of the bolt. The compressed driving spring pushes the bolt forward where it contacts the first cartridge in the magazine. The cartridge base is first contacted by the extractor and pushed forward out of the magazine. As the cartridge is driven into the chamber it begins to drag against the chamber walls, causing the extractor claw to ride outward and snap in over the cartridge rim.

The prominent firing pin now contacts the primer to ignite the propellant. The still-moving bolt is stopped and blown back, where a fixed ejector taps the expended casing out of the ejection port on the right side of the receiver tube. As long as the trigger is held down and there is ammo in the magazine, the gun will continue to shoot. When the trigger is released the sear rides back up under spring power to catch the bolt.

With the notable exception of loading the snail drums, all the various functions associated with loading and firing the MP18 are easily accomplished and require little specialised training. It is apparent that the human element was carefully considered by Schmeisser in his design and layout of the gun. The MP18/I fires at a smooth and leisurely 400 rounds per minute, or less than seven rounds per second (with practice, single shots can easily be touched off). As mentioned, the weight of the receiver and stock keep the point of aim very stable despite the cycling of the bolt. There is little muzzle blast, and earplugs are not required for comfortable shooting. This is relatively important to infantrymen, who need to be able to hear what's going on around them at all times - before and after shooting. (The Soviet PPSh-41 sub-machine gun, for example, produces an ear-splitting sonic blast which quickly destroys the shooter's hearing over a wide range.)

We put approximately 400 rounds through the gun during our test and photo session. Three different snail drums were available, and all performed without a hitch (but then, we hadn't been living in frozen mud for a week under intense shelling. . .) While no formal accuracy tests were conducted, it was quite easy to dance a tin can around at 50 meters' range from a supported position.

TOP *Detail of the ejection port of the loaded, cocked and locked machine pistol. Note the cartridge in the feed position waiting for the bolt to run forward to chamber and fire it. This is why blowback sub-machine guns are said to operate from an "open bolt"; unfortunately this exposes the mechanism to dirt and water.*

The deep finger well on the side of the hardwood stock helps to keep fingers safely away from the cocking handle - which flies up and down its track seven times a second during firing - and from the ejection port.

Detail of the rear of the receiver showing the disassembly release catch and the rear sight. Two V-notch sights are cut in an L-piece which is flipped up or down for 100m or 200m targets.

The front sight could be tapped left or right by the unit armourer when zeroing on the range, but there was no other provision for windage adjustment. Note the matching serial numbers and the ventilation holes of the barrel front support collar, which was threaded to the barrel jacket.

Ammunition

A word or two about the ballistics and lethality of the 9mm Parabellum pistol cartridge are in order here. Although it is propelled at a brisk 1,362fps, its 128 - grain .38 calibre full metal jacket bullet has poor "knockdown" properties - in blunter terms, this means simply that when it hits a human body it does relatively little damage unless it hits bone. Numerous battle accounts from both wars verify that multiple hits are required with this category of ammunition before a determined enemy soldier is put out of action. This can introduce the gunner to the (literally) nightmare experience of seeing his antagonist keep coming at him - and even shooting - despite taking a burst or two in the torso.

Conclusion

All told, the MP18/I is too big, too heavy, too awkward, and unsafe. But it is also hardy, accurate, and - by the standards of the day - exceptionally easy to make and to maintain. Many trade-offs have been made in one way or another during the subsequent eight decades of sub-machine gun development, but all are variations on a theme first composed by the genius of Hugo Schmeisser.

Credits

Gun owner, Robert Jensen, Wichita, KS; gunner, Guy Richards, Tucker, GA; uniforms & equipment, George Petersen, National Capitol Historical Sales, Springfield, VA, & Karl Schneide, Washington, DC. Special thanks to WWI historian Mike Knapp, Falls Church, VA; Rick Keller, Great War Militaria, Chambersburg, PA, & Don Thomas, Marietta, GA. Primary research sources: Nelson, Thomas, & Lockhoven, Hans, *The World's Submachine Guns (Machine Pistols), Vol.1* .

Firing the MP18/I from the shoulder in a standing position demands strength and steadiness; the ungainly 2.35lb magazine mounted on the side "like a brick on a stick" unbalances a weapon that is already heavier than the standard infantry rifle of the period.

Shooting from the hip is more comfortable, but less accurate. The relatively long barrel housing gives an adequate visual clue to the gunner's peripheral vision, and bursts can be "walked" on to the target. Muzzle blast is quite mild and does not immediately impair hearing.

Excellent results were obtained in firing from a prone, unsupported position. Rate of fire is a manageable 400 rounds per minute, and with an 8in barrel the accuracy is splendid out to a realistic battle range of around 50 yards.

It shouldn't take a tactical genius to figure out that the prone, supported position is not only the most effective, but also safest for the gunner in combat. The speed of the camera shutter has frozen the cycling bolt handle at the rear of its track, but note four ejected cases dancing in the air around the gunner's hands - the MP is in mid-burst.

STRIPPING THE MP18/I

Remove the magazine and check that there is no cartridge in the chamber. While holding the bolt cocking handle, press the trigger and allow the bolt to ride forward under control.

Press in the disassembly catch and tilt the rear of the receiver upward.

Press inward on the receiver cap, rotate it one quarter turn to the left (note interrupted threads on the receiver), and remove. Withdraw the recoil spring from the receiver.

Pull back on the bolt handle and rotate it downward to slide all the way out of its slot.

Field strip layout. *The efficient simplicity of the world's first wartime production sub-machine gun can be appreciated by the small number of parts and their ease of disassembly for repair and maintenance. (Top to bottom, left to right): Barrel, receiver and stock groups; bolt, operating/recoil spring; magazine, adaptor sleeve, dust cover.*

Cleaning and inspecting the gun is greatly simplified by its hinged receiver.

The 1908 "Light Model" Vickers, posed in 1911 to demonstrate its reduced weight - this Vickers employee must have been a strong man to give this effortless impression. By inverting the Maxim lock, thinning the receiver components and making extensive use of aluminium and steel alloy in place of brass Vickers cut the actual gun's weight to 32lbs (14.5kg), though this commercial tripod mount must increase the total significantly. (NARA)

VICKERS Mk I

"The evolution of machine gun tactics is, perhaps, the most outstanding feature of the whole war. From being, as it was considered four years ago, merely an emergency weapon or. . .'weapon of opportunity,' it has become the most important single weapon in use in any army, not even excepting artillery. A properly directed machine gun barrage is far more difficult to traverse than anything the artillery can put down and the combination of artillery and machine guns, working together, whether on the offensive or defensive, represents the highest point ever attained in the effective use of fire in battle." (Capt.Herbert McBride, 21st Bn. Canadian Expeditionary Force, *The Emma Gees*, 1918)

The calibre .303in Vickers gun, officially adopted by the British Army in 1912, remained in service for over half a century before being declared obsolete - regretfully - in 1968. During faithful service in two World Wars and countless lesser campaigns this simplified and lightened version of the Maxim performed legendary feats of endurance, earning the respect and admiration of the Tommies who used it and the fear and loathing of their enemies.

Development

In 1892 British industrialist Alfred Vickers bought out the Maxim-Nordenfeldt Company, continuing their production of Hiram Maxim's heavy machine gun for export worldwide. In response to requests from the British military - dissatisfied with the considerable weight and complexity of their small number of early production Maxims - engineers at the new Vickers Sons & Maxim Ltd. began at the turn of the century to simplify and lighten the gun while retaining its basic mechanism and configuration.

The models of 1901 and 1906 produced under the direction of engineer George Buckham were a long step in the right direction, primarily due to his inverting the "knee break" of the lock connector, using previously wasted space and thus allowing the height of the heavy steel box receiver to be reduced by two inches all around. Other weight-saving measures included replacing the heavy brass water jacket with one of thin steel corrugated for strength, and machining away excess metal everywhere else on the gun. The Maxim's elaborate method of depositing empty cartridges into a tube for front ejection was also discarded: now they simply and efficiently dropped through a rectangular hole in the bottom of the receiver, fitted with a sliding dust cover.

By 1908 the gun had been lightened to the point where nearly half the 60lb (27.2kg) weight of the original Maxim had been eliminated. Mechanical refinements included the very desirable ability to adjust headspace, and introduction of a muzzle booster. The resulting Model 1908 "Light Pattern" Vickers was favourably received in formal trials beginning in 1910, culminating in official adoption of the "Gun, Machine,.303, Mark I" in November 1912.

The Machine Gun Corps

Despite the original Maxim gun's long record of success in British colonial wars and the enthusiastic reception of the lighter Vickers, conservative generals and a parsimonious War Office considered existing stocks of Maxims to be sufficient for the time being. While the German Army was moving forward quickly with its

BELOW RIGHT *The key to the lightened Vickers was in its inverted Maxim lock, the previously unused space in the top of the receiver accommodating the breaking action of the toggle joint. These engineering drawings show the mechanism at the positions of partial extraction, and full recoil; note in the latter drawing how the face of the lock is cammed down to eject the spent cartridge and align a new one with the chamber. From* Handbook of the Vickers Machine Gun Model of 1915, *US Army Ordnance Corps, 1917. (Author's collection)*

BELOW *Detail of the lock mechanism showing position of the cartridges in operation: the top round would still be in the feed belt and the bottom round would be chambered and ready to fire when the lock is fully forward. On firing, the lock moves rearward under recoil to simultaneously extract the top round from the belt and the empty casing from the chamber for ejection. (**Caution** - we used dummy rounds for this dangerous photo set-up; there is a distinct risk of accidental discharge of the lower cartridge.)*

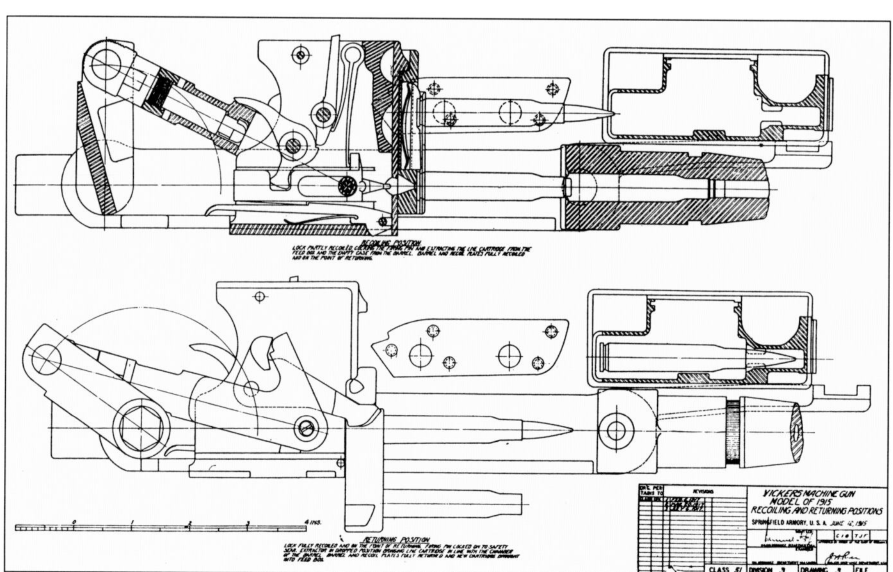

Reconstruction - Battle of the Aisne, May 1918: The crew of a British Army Vickers Mk I emplaced in second-line trenches. Viewed from the front they would be dangerously exposed to German sniper and counter-machine gun fire if they were in the forward trench, but this emplacement is several hundred yards behind. Their primary mission, usually executed at night, is indirect fire on German support elements in the rear; during daylight hours their secondary mission is direct suppressive fire - which the position of the sights indicates here.

The No.1 (gunner) wears the distinctive gunner's "waistcoat", made from doubled uniform cloth with characteristic leather shoulder pads for protection when carrying the tripod or gun. He and his No.2 both wear the "small box respirator" or gas mask, as a yellow cloud of poison gas from enemy shells rolls towards them. Ammunition and gun parts exposed to gas quickly corroded, making them unusable until thoroughly cleaned; chlorine, in particular, left a thin film on the ammunition which would foul the chamber so badly that within a hundred rounds the cartridges would not feed.

France, 1918: a British MGC sergeant conducts a training session on the Vickers Mk I for newly-arrived AEF "Doughboys". American formations assigned to British and French sectors of the front were armed with the machine guns of their "host" armies to simplify supply and tactical employment. Note - in contrast to the gun in our colour photos - the straight connection of the hose into the underside of the jacket behind the muzzle, leading to a condenser bag in the background. (NARA)

acquisition programme, all but 100 of the less than 2,000 heavy machine guns with which the British Army went to war in 1914 were the old .303in Maxims. As late as April 1915 Gen.Sir Douglas Haig, GOC British 1st Army in France who went on to command the whole British Expeditionary Force, notoriously commented that "The machine gun is a much overrated weapon and two per battalion is more than sufficient." The realities of trench warfare were soon brought home to the War Office, however, and the Vickers was ordered into full scale production.

The wholly inadequate section of two guns per infantry battalion or cavalry regiment was soon doubled; and the efficient employment of machine guns grew exponentially with establishment of a separate Machine Gun Corps in October 1915. This separation from the infantry was valuable in building prestige and esprit de corps, but also in providing a highly supportive environment for development of the science of machine gunnery. By mid-1916 the MGC had some 4,000 officers and 80,000 men; and three 16-gun MGC companies were available to each three-brigade, 12-battalion division. The introduction of the high-powered Mk VIIZ round had also increased the Vickers' maximum range to about 3,500 yards.

By early 1918 reorganisation of the infantry division and supporting MGC companies at brigade and divisional level gave each division 64 Vickers guns. This meant that, with eight of a division's now nine infantry battalions usually in the trenches at any one time, the effective concentration was eight heavy machine guns per battalion. By the armistice of November 1918 more than 73,600 new Vickers guns had been delivered, with about 5,000 in service at any given time.

Due to the army system of emphasised phonetic pronunciation of the letters of the alphabet, the members of the elite brotherhood of machine gunners became known as the "Emma-Gees." Wisely, the British allowed the Emma Gees - a self-described "Suicide Club", due to the furious return fire which they often drew on themselves - to remain separate from the tactical control of local infantry commanders. Instead, specially trained officers and their highly proficient crews were able to site their guns to maximum advantage both to defend against assault and to rain death on enemy positions both front and rear. The men who made up the Machine Gun Corps were among the best in the British Army; the following passage from Capt.E.J.Solano's 1917 manual *Machine Gun Training* sets out the ideal:

"Qualities of Machine Gunners: Soldiers selected for duty with a machine gun section should possess, as far as possible, the following qualifications: good physique, good eyesight, calm temperament, fair education, mechanical aptitude. It is most important that men selected for the machine gun section should remain with it as long as possible, in order that they may acquire a high standard of skill. Young soldiers of about a year's service are therefore the most suitable for selection."

The Vickers immortalised in the cap badge of the Machine Gun Corps. Although the MGC was disbanded in 1922, a number of infantry battalions (e.g. those of the Middlesex Regiment) were converted to heavy MG units from 1936, and World War II divisions each included one of these battalions.

This last was a bit optimistic, given the depressingly short life expectancy of both infantrymen and machine gunners in the trenches (during the war the overall casualty rate among British troops sent overseas was about one man in three killed or wounded). Replacements pouring out of the intensive six week course at the major training schools at Camiers and Grantham were soon lost in battle. The Machine Gun Corps' average wartime strength was 71,000, never quite meeting the fierce demand for qualified officers and men.

The understandable objections of the infantry to the siphoning off of talent and the sometimes annoying independence of the Machine Gun Corps was at least partially overcome when the excellent Lewis light machine gun began reaching front line infantry in quantity in 1916. Its issue finally reached the figure of 36 per battalion - two per rifle platoon plus four in battalion headquarters. This partnership

Well-known photograph of Mk I Vickers crew during the Battle of the Somme, July 1916; the slight blurring of the belt shows that the gun is actually firing. Both crewmen wear the primitive Phenate-Hexamine anti-gas helmet, and No.1 has the special padded waistcoat. The gun is fitted with the short-lived Sangster auxiliary tripod intended for rapid expedient use, its legs strapped up under the barrel jacket. The legs of the standard Mk IV tripod are securely sandbagged for extra stability. (NARA)

of light, quick reaction firepower under infantry control at every level, and heavy, sustained, supporting firepower out to extreme range, eventually proved to be a winning combination.

Indirect fire

With modern "general purpose" machine guns almost always used for direct fire, it is interesting to note the extensive use of heavy machine guns in the past as indirect fire weapons, much as mortars are used today; this technique is discussed in the Introduction. Even without a forward observer to spot and correct the beaten zone of fire, a battery of heavy water-cooled guns could be aimed using the principles of geometry in the manner of traditional artillery, doing extraordinary damage over a wide area. Demonstrations for visiting VIPs were regularly set up by the main British machine gunnery schools at Grantham and Camiers: guns hidden so far away as to be almost inaudible on firing would cause the barren earth in front of the reviewing stand to erupt in a miniature storm. It was a dull man indeed who could witness this without a shudder of horror at the thought of infantry having to traverse areas under such fire; and one is tempted to wonder how many senior staff officers actually saw and absorbed these lessons.

This war was the first real test of the machine gun, and hundreds of thousands were employed under the most arduous conditions imaginable. The most oft-quoted example of the Vickers' dependability came on 24 August 1916 during the first battle of the Somme, and was glowingly recounted in Lt.Col.G.S. Hutchison's *Machine Guns* (1938):

"A somewhat amazing exploit was carried out by the 100th Machine Gun Company. Ten guns were grouped in Savoy Trench, from which a magnificent view was obtained of the German line at a range of about 2,000 yards. Two companies of infantry were lent for the purpose of carrying ammunition and water to the battery position during the previous night, when the machine guns were installed, and camouflaged with netting. The operation orders read that 'rapid fire is to be maintained continuously for twelve hours, to cover the attack and consolidation.'

"The 100th Infantry Brigade had been engaged in the first assault upon High Wood on the 16th July, an attack which was repulsed with heaviest losses, due largely to lack of artillery preparation and support. For the new assault, with limited objectives, the brigadier was determined that nothing should be lacking in effective covering fire. It is to the credit of the gunners and the Vickers itself that the orders were fulfilled to the letter.

"During the attack on the 24th August, 250 rounds short of one million were fired by the ten guns. Four 2-gallon petrol tins of water [per gun, surely?], *the company's water bottles, and all the urine tins from the neighbourhood were emptied into the guns for cooling purposes, an illustration of the amount of water consumed; while a party was employed throughout the action carrying ammunition. Strict discipline as to barrel-changing was maintained. The company artificer, assisted by one private, maintained a belt-loading machine in action without cessation for twelve hours. A prize of five francs to each of the members of the gun-team firing the greatest number of rounds was secured by Sergeant P.Dean, DCM, with a record of just over 120,000 rounds.*

"The action was a remarkable performance in itself, if prodigal in its expenditure of ammunition. Nevertheless, the assault was a brilliant success, the opera-

France, June 1918: at Corps level Vickers guns were available in MGC Motor Batteries, mounted on Vickers-Clyno motorcycle combinations. While it was possible to fire the gun while mounted, they were normally driven into a staging area, dismounted, then man-packed up to the fighting line. (NARA)

The "Cone, front, muzzle attachment Mk II" is a classic muzzle booster device, trapping and diverting propellant gas to drive the recoiling parts back sharply, raising the rate of fire and increasing reliability. The right-angled hose connection here is a postwar addition.

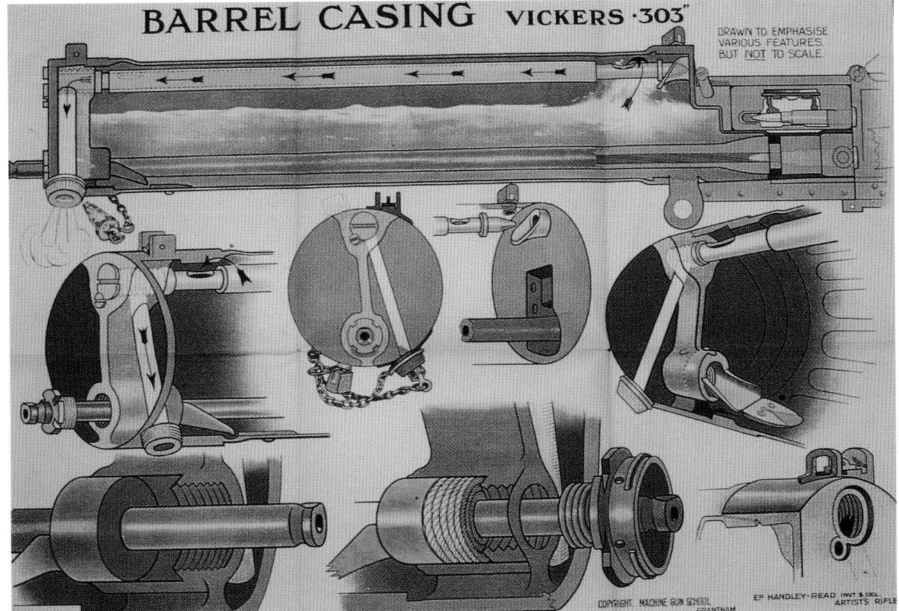

Cutaways of the barrel jacket, from a series of beautifully drawn diagrams by Edward Handley-Read of the Artist's Rifles, originally prepared for the British Army MG School at Grantham. Note the sleeve fitted to the valve tube, sliding up or back depending on the elevation or depression of the muzzle; this stops water escaping from the jacket when the gun is in operation or being carried. Oiled asbestos string packing is wound on the rear of the barrel and on the muzzle gland to keep water in. Ramps are thoughtfully provided as guides when replacing the steam tube and the barrel, a useful feature for crews operating under stress. (US Army Military History Institute, Carlisle Barracks, PA - USAMHI)

Water jacket filler hole. Water was often scarce in combat, and there are many references to a hard-pressed crew having to use urine instead. (This is not the only reason for scepticism about the tales of crews using boiling water from the jacket to brew tea - unless they liked the flavour of mineral oil, cordite and rust. . .)

tions being difficult, and all objectives being taken within a short time. The machine gunners sustained one casualty, while prisoners examined at both divisional and corps headquarters reported that 'the effect of the machine-gun barrage was annihilating. Counter attacks endeavouring to retake the ground lost were broken up whilst being concentrated east of the Flers Ridge and High Wood.' "

The American Vickers

After lengthy testing of the lightened Vickers, the US Army finally adopted it in American .30-06 calibre as the "Vickers Machine Gun, Model of 1915." The basis of issue was to be a generous six guns for each infantry MG company or cavalry MG troop. An initial production contract for 125 guns was placed in November 1915 with Colt's under license from Vickers. A year later an additional order for 4,000 guns was also placed - despite such severe start-up problems at Colt's that not a single satisfactory gun had yet been delivered. Scandalously, when America entered the war on 6 April 1917 there were only 1,305 machine guns on hand, most of which were Model 1909 Benét-Mercié machine rifles, with a few US Model 1904 Maxims.

It was not until August 1917 that the first few Colt-made Vickers guns were delivered. A desperate British order for 6,000 guns could not be filled before the end of the war, but at least some much-needed spare parts were eventually provided. Development of John Browning's Model 1917 heavy machine gun, an even simpler and lighter design than the Vickers, stopped further production at Colt's. Interestingly, over 7,000 of the American calibre Vickers guns were brought out of storage at the beginning of World War II and sent to Britain in urgent response to the disaster at Dunkirk.

The first 12 American divisions arriving in France were equipped with Hotchkiss guns, and the next ten with British-made Vickers guns; this was necessary not only because of the US Army's critical shortage of machine guns, but in the interests of commonality of training, tactical employment, and resupply.

Identification plate on the rear tripod leg revealing this to be a very early model: "TRIPOD, .303 MAXIM, MARK IV". The coiled leather strap is used to secure the legs when folded for transport.

LEFT AND RIGHT *Views of the Mk IV tripod. Relatively light compared to its more massive and elaborate German counterpart, it was still necessarily heavy in order to provide a stable mount for safety in overhead firing and indirect fire accuracy.*

Detail of a Vickers Mk IV tripod fitted with the "Dial, traversing, Mk II", allowing accurate laying of the gun on pre-registered targets; and of the original style feed belt with extended brass spacers every three rounds.

Vickers Mk I Technical Specifications

Nomenclature	Gun, Machine, .303, Mark I
Manufacturer	Vickers Ltd., Crayford and Erith
Calibre	.303in (7.62mm)
Ammunition	Mk VII & VIIZ ball; tracer; blank
System of operation	Short recoil
Cooling	Water; jacket capacity 7 to 10 pints (3.9 to 5.6 liters)
Selector	None; full automatic only
Feed	250-round cloth belts
Length	45.5ins (1155.7mm)
Weight, gun	40lbs 6oz (18.3kg) with water
Weight, Mk IV tripod	50lbs (22.6kg)
Barrel	28.5ins (647.7mm); 5 grooves, left twist
Sights	Post front, aperture rear on leaf
Rate of fire	450-500rpm cyclic
Muzzle velocity	2,440fps (744mps)
Max.range	2,900 yards (Mk VII), 3,500 (Mk VIIZ)

Detail of the elevating handwheel and reference scale on the Mk IV tripod; it is marked in increments of five minutes of angle, so that one full turn raises or lowers the muzzle by four degrees.

Mechanism

Although a marked improvement over the Maxim, the Vickers was not without its faults. The most obvious of these was the weight of the gun, tripod and associated equipment, ammunition, and spares. While water cooling was necessary for true sustained fire, this gave away the gun position with a plume of steam when it boiled, and tended to freeze and rupture the water jacket in severe winter weather. According to contemporary accounts water in the jacket boils after 500 to 600 rounds, then evaporates at a rate of 1.5 pints per 1,000 rounds. Even in Europe water may have to be carried some distance by resupply parties, making this a serious tactical concern.

The complexity of the mechanism and the precise adjustments that must be

The receiver. The crank handle flips back and forth in an arc during firing; its position (here, normal for a loaded gun) is the cue to probable causes when a stoppage occurs, and crews were endlessly drilled to take the prescribed immediate action.

ABOVE LEFT *Spade grips and trigger mechanism on the "rear crosspiece." The inverted U-shaped safety bar must be pulled up against spring pressure before the oval trigger plate can be pushed in. The rear sight is marked from 100 to 2,900 yards in 100 yard increments (although nearly identical to that on Great War guns, its aperture within a protective window identifies this sight as a postwar Mk IV).*

ABOVE RIGHT *The V-shaped cut above the port in the feed block allows the No.2 to quickly retract the belt-holding pawls - note grooved tabs - and remove the belt (here an example with spacers but lacking the usual extensions).*

Wooden 250-round ammunition boxes soon proved inadequate for the harsh environment of the trenches, and were eventually replaced by galvanised metal tins with looped leather or webbing handles.

made to ensure efficient operation meant that crews had to be highly trained - a relatively long and costly process. One small example is the fusee spring tension, which must be individually gauged on each gun to ensure smooth return of the locking mechanism to feed and fire; this is accomplished with a pull-type spring scale which is just one small part of each gun's elaborate tool kit. Instruction manuals list pages of malfunctions with suggestions on how to identify and rectify each of them.

Although the Vickers is essentially similar to the already described Maxim Maschinengewehr, there are sufficient differences to warrant a detailed tour from muzzle to grips.

The muzzle booster

The "Cone, front, muzzle attachment, Mk II" was an improvement over earlier models, adopted in 1916. It operates by catching a proportion of the propellant gas accompanying the firing of each round in a cone and deflecting it into a cup attached to the barrel. This provides impulse to ensure movement of the recoiling parts even when the gun is dirty, nearly frozen, or heavily fouled with carbon. Although very efficient, unfortunate consequences of its design include excessive side blast, discomforting to the crew No.2; and the need to unscrew the cup before the barrel can be removed and replaced. In conditions where it was unsafe for No.2 to crawl forward and do the job the whole gun had to be dismounted and pulled under cover.

The water jacket

"And how that water does boil away! In spite of the most careful use of the condenser, it evaporates at a rapid rate and then the problem is how to replenish it. Even though the action may be literally on the bank of a river it may be an impossible task to go the few feet and back; and, often, on the soggy, rain-drenched fields of Flanders, where everything was simply soaked, not enough real water could be procured to fill the jacket. More than a few times the members of the gun crew have been called upon to 'make water,' and there is a sort of grim humour in the fact that on such occasions few, if any, could produce the goods. . .". So wrote Capt.Herbert McBride, a Great War machine gunner with the famous Canadian 21st Battalion, in his 1935 book *A Rifleman Went to War*.

Apart from being corrugated, the Vickers' steel water jacket is virtually identical in form and function to that of its predecessor the Maxim. Its inner workings may be mysterious to those who haven't been able to peer inside, but the beautiful diagrams prepared for the Grantham MG School by Edward Handley-Read lift the veil (see p.61). The barrel is submerged in water, to which it transfers heat during firing. The water begins to boil after some 500 to 600 rounds of rapid fire; steam finds its way through ports at the front or back of the valve tube, to escape through a port underneath the muzzle. A detachable rubber hose is normally fitted to this while the gun is operating, directing the steam into some suitable container of water; if the end of the hose is under the surface much of the steam immediately condenses back into water, which can be poured back into the jacket from the container (some people have a vague but mistaken impression that the water circulates back into the gun automatically).

Despite the efficient cooling system barrels still needed to be replaced after some 10,000 to 12,000 rounds - half that, as a safety measure, during overhead fire above friendly troops. To avoid draining the water a cork stopper is quickly popped into the front hole of the jacket by No.2 as No.1 slides the "recoiling parts" out the back, while lowering the muzzle to keep water from escaping into the receiver; the cork is automatically knocked out when the new barrel slides into position. A few turns of the muzzle end cup and casing have the gun back in action in less than two minutes if the crew is experienced.

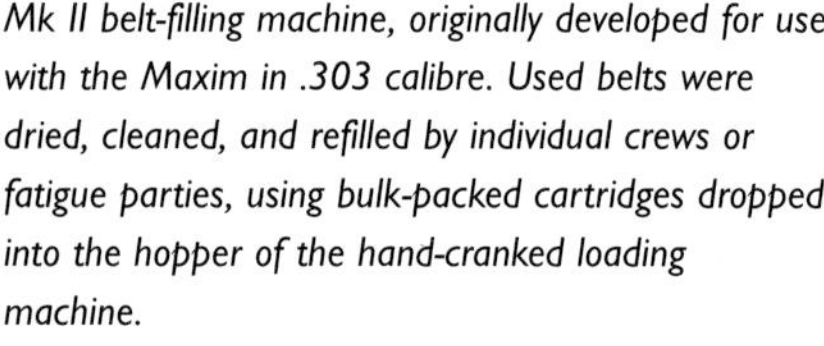

Mk II belt-filling machine, originally developed for use with the Maxim in .303 calibre. Used belts were dried, cleaned, and refilled by individual crews or fatigue parties, using bulk-packed cartridges dropped into the hopper of the hand-cranked loading machine.

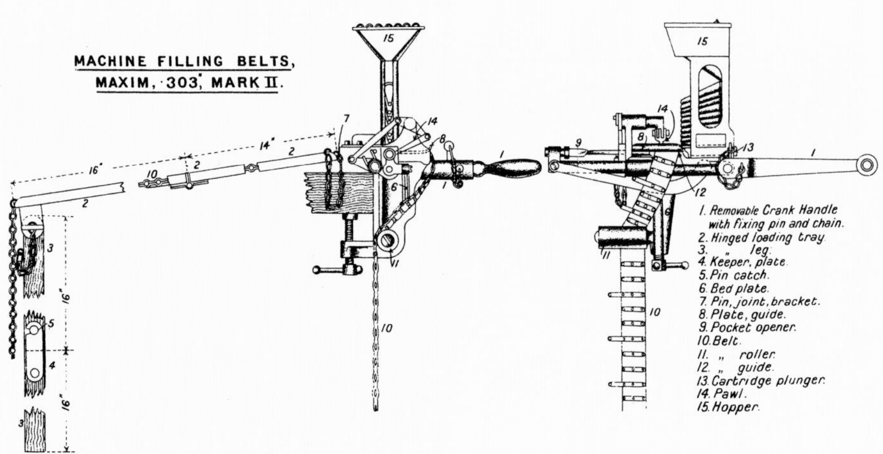

Firing the Vickers Mk I: the antique belt with brass spacers has been discarded for a "stripless" belt of postwar streamlined Mk VIIIZ ammunition, in this case 1953 production cartridges straight from a sealed tin. A pair of "Huns" are caught in the stream of bullets at nearly point blank range, just 150 yards away. Fired in short bursts at 500rpm cyclic, the "hot" Mk VIIIZ bullets streak out at over 2,550 fps, tearing the targets apart. At this range the improved 1916 Mk VIIZ rounds would penetrate 6ft 8ins (2m) of turf, 2ft 6ins (.76m) of sand, or 1ft 6ins (.45m) of oak.

Steady on its tripod and dropping its empties through a slot underneath the receiver, the primary visual indication that the Vickers is being fired is a fine cloud of dust kicked up from sandbags and surrounding earth by the shock wave at the muzzle.

Interestingly, the German practice of providing armour protection to the water jacket was not followed with the Vickers; although some experimental shields were made during 1915-16 they were not fielded. It is also puzzling that no standard hole patching kits, jacket heaters or covers were issued until years after the World War. Various flash hiders were tried out during the war, including a large, flared stovepipe design that slipped over the whole jacket. None proved worthwhile, and close night firing was often inefficiently screened by a curtain of dampened sandbags hung a few yards in front of the muzzle.

The tripod mount

The "Mounting, tripod, MG, Mk IV" dates back to 1906 and was used with the .303in Maxim. Although a considerable improvement over its awkward, heavy predecessors, it sacrificed accuracy for simplicity. Weighing some 50lbs (22.6kg), the Mk IV was finely adjustable for elevation using a handwheel and worm gear, but lacked a mechanical traversing mechanism. The increasing use of the Vickers for precise indirect fire during the war led to installation of graduated scales on the handwheel and the mounting socket, enabling the gunner to engage predetermined targets without direct observation by "dialing up" settings previously recorded in a notebook or on a range card.

Some smaller, lighter tripods and bipods were cobbled together and used in limited numbers with the aim of increasing the portability of the gun. This became largely unnecessary as great numbers of the light Lewis guns were brought into the forward trenches, allowing the heavier Vickers to be positioned further back. In the absence of a standardised version any number of expedient anti-aircraft mounts were devised at unit level; some were fitted with a rectangular metal strip basket for an ammo box.

A massive and complicated mount for semi-permanent use in prepared positions appeared in 1917. Weighing more than 100lbs, and including an ammo box holder, it pivoted at the muzzle in order to present the smallest possible target, while allowing a 77 degree arc of fire. Use of this mount in the confined space of pillboxes led to development of a pear-shaped blast deflector to push out the noxious fumes from burned propellant.

The need to fire over trench parapets without exposing the gunner led to several combination periscope and remote triggering devices. Popularly known as "hyposcopes", they are said to have proved unsatisfactory.

The receiver

Almost indestructably built by riveting thick steel plates into a rectangular box, the size of the Vickers' receiver had been reduced substantially by modification of the Maxim's locking mechanism. This gave both a welcome reduction in overall weight and a slimmer outline. In contrast to most other guns with complicated machining inside, the Vickers receiver serves primarily as a receptacle for the recoiling parts and other major groupings. The "recoiling parts" are the heart of the gun, so named because they are physically connected and act in concert, sliding back and forth upon detonation of each round. They consist of the barrel, sideplates, lock, crank assembly and fusee spring assembly. Other main groupings include the feed block, rear crosspiece (backplate), and two piece cover with attached rear sight. These, of course, are where the slow, precise and expensive machining operations are needed and where an almost endless array of possible malfunctions require so much specialised training.

The last few empty pockets of a cloth belt blur into the receiver; note the blackening of the sandbag under the muzzle.

The spade grips

As with the MG08, the twin wooden handles on the backplate are swollen at the centre for comfort, hollowed out for oil bottles and capped with a brush applicator. The prominent "firing plate" or trigger is protected from firing by the necessity of first lifting a spring-loaded inverted U-shaped safety bar. The whole assembly is easily removable, and could be simply replaced with a modified version for aircraft and tank installations.

The sights

The sights are off-set to the left, rather awkwardly, as the dominant eye is commonly the right. This leads to a bit of neck-craning to align the head while sitting directly behind the gun, or the need to sit off-centre. The rear sight assembly is of the tangent style, consisting of a fixed aperture battlesight set for 400 yards and a slender swing-up leaf. World War I guns have indicator plates calibrated for Mk VII ammunition and are marked in 100-yard increments from 100 to 2,900 yards. Adjustment is by a drum knob turning a toothed gear so that it climbs the leaf. Originally an open U-notch, it was soon converted to the more precise aperture style. The rear sight is not adjustable for windage.

The front sight is a semi-fixed rectangular blade post, well protected by a pair of metal "ears" welded to the water jacket. The central blade can be tapped left or right by an armourer to zero the gun on the range. In common with all other sights of this type, however, the taller vertical ears can easily be confused with the sight post in high stress situations, leading to significant aiming error. A large oval-shaped anti-aircraft front sight was also issued, clamping onto the water jacket with a ring; it was most efficiently used in conjunction with a special clip-on rear sight with a larger than normal aperture for quick target acquisition.

Accessories

Arguably the most important accessories are the gunner's kits. From the small leather gunner's pouch with a few critical spares and tools, to the heavy wooden armourer's chest filled with enough tools and parts for the complete care and feeding of a multi-gun platoon, these are an absolute necessity. Other early issue items include canvas bags for condensing water, originally regulation horse feedbags; these were later replaced by "blivet" bags specifically designed for machine gun use. They were quickly replaced by two-gallon metal petrol cans; although flimsy, these served well enough.

Boxes, belts and bad ammo

Ammunition boxes, each holding one belt of 250 rounds, went through some practical evolution early in the war. The original Maxim type teak (and later pine) boxes, beautifully crafted with intricate dovetail joints, almost immediately proved inadequate in the trenches, which demanded something sturdier, cheaper, and waterproof. They were soon replaced by galvanised metal boxes with double hinged lids and leather handles. These were made gas-proof by addition of felt inside the lid, and reinforced with a metal band around its upper rim. The most common box in the Great War, the No.8 Mk I standardised in 1916, weighed nearly 22lbs fully loaded.

The cotton canvas belts themselves remained essentially unchanged during the war. Brass spacers were riveted between each cartridge pocket, with every third spacer extended to mark the depth to which all pockets should be loaded.

These spacers also served to keep loaded cartridges from being knocked out of position when the belts were roughly bounced around in the boxes.

Ammunition was normally issued in bulk and cartridges had to be individually loaded into belts. While this could be done by hand, belt-loading machines were issued with each gun and usually kept on the gun cart. The Mk II was a hand-cranked device that fed cartridges from a hopper into pockets in the belt. Weighing over 20lbs, it was slow and tedious to use and belt-filling was considered a punishment chore by most crewmen. Wartime experiments with preloaded disposable stripless belts showed promise, but had to wait until the eve of World War II before gaining official favour.

As previously noted, cloth belts are notoriously inefficient under combat conditions. Subject to shrinkage or expansion from moisture, they rot, mildew, tear, fray and freeze depending on the prevailing conditions. Crew members had to constantly check their ammunition belts, often twisting each round periodically to keep it from sticking and damaging lockfaces. Several types of metal belts were tested, the most successful being a non-disintegrating model patented by Thomas Sangster in 1915. Alas, this too had its own problems and was not widely used. British gunners finished the war using essentially the same type of belt as Hiram Maxim first fired in his 1883 prototype.

A particularly unfortunate episode occurred with the first deliveries of urgently needed .303in cartridges made in America. Units receiving them immediately began reporting an enormous number of stoppages, primarily due to case separations. It was soon determined that the brass cartridge cases had been improperly "drawn" in the manufacturing process, leading to blown out bases; and that rim thickness did not meet necessary standards of consistency. This disturbing development increased the severity of small arms ammunition shortages as millions of cartridges proved suitable only for rifle training.

Firing the Vickers

Appropriately, our live fire session with the Vickers was conducted on the same day as that with the Lewis, giving us the opportunity to reflect on the unique strengths of each gun as used in the trenches, and the way their weaknesses were largely compensated for by changes in tactical doctrine.

The trench complex at Shimpstown, PA, formerly used by the Great War Association for its "living history" re-enactments, provided the right touch of authenticity on an overcast September day. Well-known machine gun builder and dealer Charles Erb provided a World War I production Mk I up-graded with some postwar fittings; he, gunner Gus Knapp, assistant gunner Steve Altemus and location assistant John Exley all pitched in to build a semi-protected indirect fire position such as would be found in second or third line trenches well behind the front line. Carrying 35lbs (15.8kg) of dry gun, 50lbs (22.6kg) of tripod, plus ammunition and water a mere quarter mile over dry ground - and not under fire - provided a very mild lesson in the realities of life on the Western Front. The tripod was set in position by the No.1, the gun quickly attached by the No.2, and No.3 placed the cans of ammo and water. Had additional members of the regulation four- to six-man team been present they would have brought up more ammunition, spare barrels, tools, water and provisions.

Erb set about installing the lock, verifying the correct 7-9lb tension of the fusee spring, filling the water jacket, and loading an old brass-spacer belt with cartridges for photography. The fragile 75-year-old belt was then removed so that the real shooting could begin. Before shooting, it is a pleasant exercise to raise the back portion of the receiver cover and watch the beautifully machined and well oiled lock mechanism run back and forth under action of the crank handle. Unlike the "jerk and slam" of modern designs, the Vickers works more like a miniature steam engine, its smoothly moving steel shafts, levers, springs and cams sliding with measured grace through their appointed tasks.

We opened a sealed tin of 1953 vintage British Mk VIIIZ high powered machine gun ammo, pre-loaded in cloth 250-round "stripless belts." Despite the airtight storage can the 44-year-old cartridges were intermittently discoloured, but otherwise as good as new. The gun is best loaded with the top cover shut. No.2 slipped the extended belt leader through the feed; No.3 grabbed it, and maintained tension as No.1 worked the crank handle through the required two cycles, chambering a round. Then, setting the rear sight at its bare minimum of 100 yards, he

used the elevating handwheel and mild taps on the receiver to bring the aperture and post dead on to a pair of cardboard "Huns."

After a moment of dramatic pause, Knapp lifted the safety bar with his second fingers and pressed the trigger with his thumbs, rousing the old Mk I to roaring life once again. Instantly the targets were enveloped in showers of dirt and shale as the burst hit directly to their front. A quick turn of the elevating handwheel brought the muzzle up, and the second short burst was right on the money. The super-hot Mk VIIIZ bullets produced an unusually large number of ricochets, identified by a loud and angry buzzing as the radically destabilised bullets tumbled end over end at supersonic speed. Again and again the Vickers blasted away, light taps on the receiver left and right sawing first one and then the other target in two.

Due to the configuration of the range area, the power of the ammunition, and the close proximity of occupied farm buildings and animals, the extreme range of this shooting test was a laughable 150 yards; the experience aroused keen curiosity about the practicalities of indirect fire out to a couple of miles.

Although you can't balance a champagne glass on the top cover when firing, the Vickers is a smoothly shooting gun, nearly as stable as the MG08. The sturdy Mk IV tripod absorbs virtually all of the recoil, and muzzle blast is quite tolerable to the gunner even without ear protection; however, the No.2 and No.3 get quite a sharp earful of blast and a noseful of nitrocellulose fumes as the recoil booster vents sideways.

Thankfully, we had no need to go through any "immediate action" drills to correct stoppages; in some 600 rounds of short and long bursts there were no problems that could not be immediately dealt with by cycling the crank handle, or poking around a bit with the top cover open. It was also appreciated that there was no need to try refilling a boiling hot water jacket, or removing and replacing the barrel within the mandatory two minutes and under pressure of an enemy attack.

For such an undeniably complicated gun field stripping is surprisingly easy, as shown in the accompanying photographs. However, compared to today's GPMGs with their quick-change barrels and "soldier-proof" mechanisms, the Old World flavour of the Vickers is quite distinct. A final test came in breaking the gun down for man-packed transport back to the cars. No matter how often it is pointed out that the Mk I is lighter by one-third than the MG08, it is still a beast to shoulder and carry over a trench parapet for a stroll across No Man's Land.

Conclusion

That the British Army kept the Vickers in service for over half a century speaks for itself. Despite the weight and complexity inseparable from its pre-Great War vintage, and the awkward limitations of water cooling, its ability to deliver accurate direct and indirect fire out to long ranges, and its practically complete reliability of function under widely varying battlefield conditions, secure its place in any list of truly great machine guns.

Credits

Gun owner and crew No.3 (ammunition carrier), Charles Erb, Fredericktown, PA; No.1 (gunner), Gus Knapp, Falls Church, VA; No.2 (assistant), Steve Altemus, Alexandria, VA; uniforms & equipment, Mike & Gus Knapp, & Great War Militaria, Chambersburg, PA; location assistant, John Exley IV, Mechanicsville, VA; range, Great War Association, Shimpstown, PA. Primary research sources: Goldsmith, Dolf, *The Grand Old Lady of No Man's Land*; Hutchison, Lt.Col.G.S., *Machine Guns*. Thanks also to Martin Pegler, HM Royal Armouries, Leeds, UK.

Our crew moves to another location; No.1 carries the 50lb (22.6kg) tripod, No.2 the 40lb (18.3kg) gun, and No.3 a water can and a woefully inadequate 500 rounds of ammunition. One or more additional riflemen/ammunition carriers were usually part of the crew.

STRIPPING THE VICKERS MK I

From the British Army manual: "On the command 'Unload', No.1 lowers the tangent sight but not the slide, turns the crank handle twice in succession onto the buffer spring, letting it fly back each time onto the check lever; then presses up the finger-pieces on the lower pawls, while No.2 withdraws and repacks the belt in the box. . ."

Lift the cover latch and raise the rear section of the double receiver cover. (Note that when the sight leaf is folded down the peep off-set to the left of its base rises into the vertical, forming a handy battle sight for fast target engagement out to 500 yards.)

Rotate the crank handle all the way to the rear; reach into the receiver and guide the lock upward.

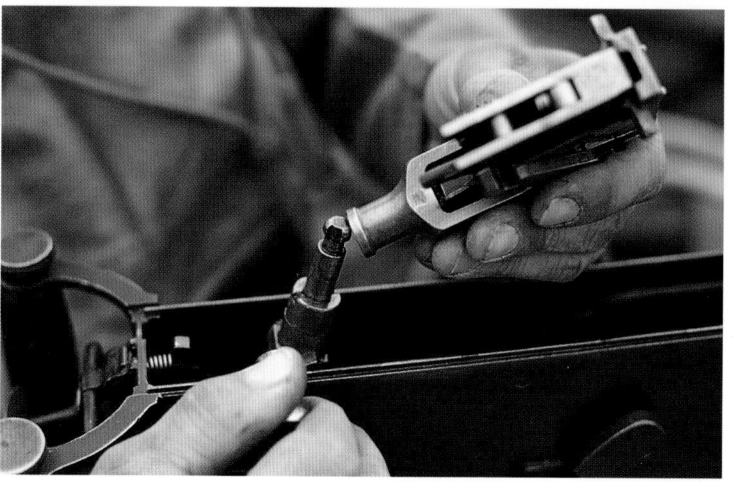

Twist the lock one-third of a turn to the right and free it from its connecting rod. Allow the crank handle to ease forward, then close the rear cover.

ABOVE *Rotate the front cover latch back and up, then raise the front (feedblock) cover.*

RIGHT *The feedblock can now be lifted straight up and out of the receiver.*

Push forward on the fusee spring cover until its fastening hooks can be disengaged from studs on the side of the receiver.

Turn the fusee until its lugs can be withdrawn through cuts in the receiver side.

Lift the rear cover once again, unscrew the T-shaped bolt, and allow the backplate and grip assembly ("rear crosspiece") to rotate downwards.

Pull out the two rear body pieces.

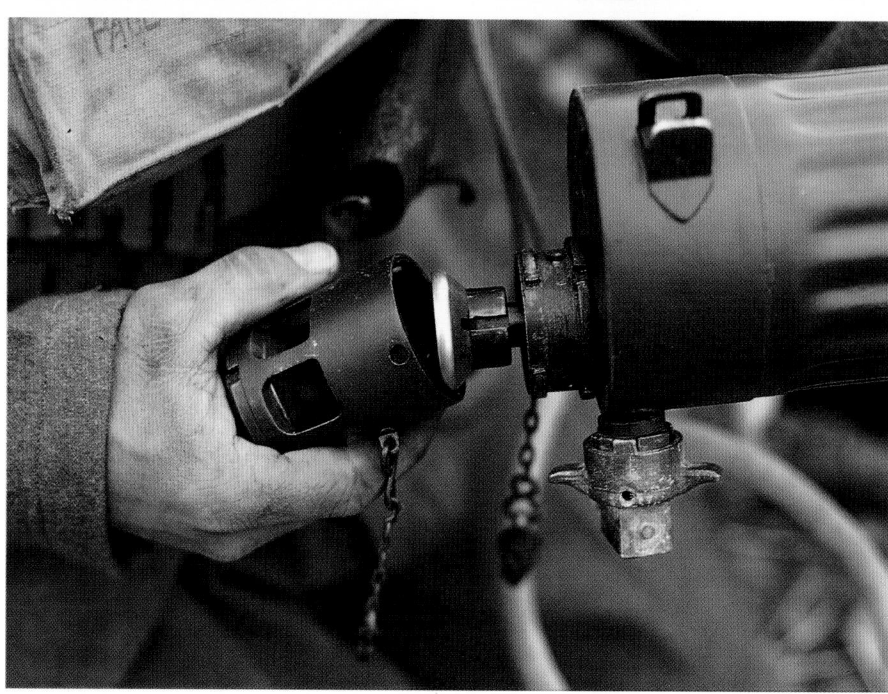

Withdraw the retaining pin from the muzzle booster assembly and remove its outer casing, exposing the muzzle cup. Next, unscrew the cup with the special spanner from the gunner's kit.

Withdraw the "recoiling parts" - the crank handle assembly, side plates and attached barrel - through the rear of the receiver.

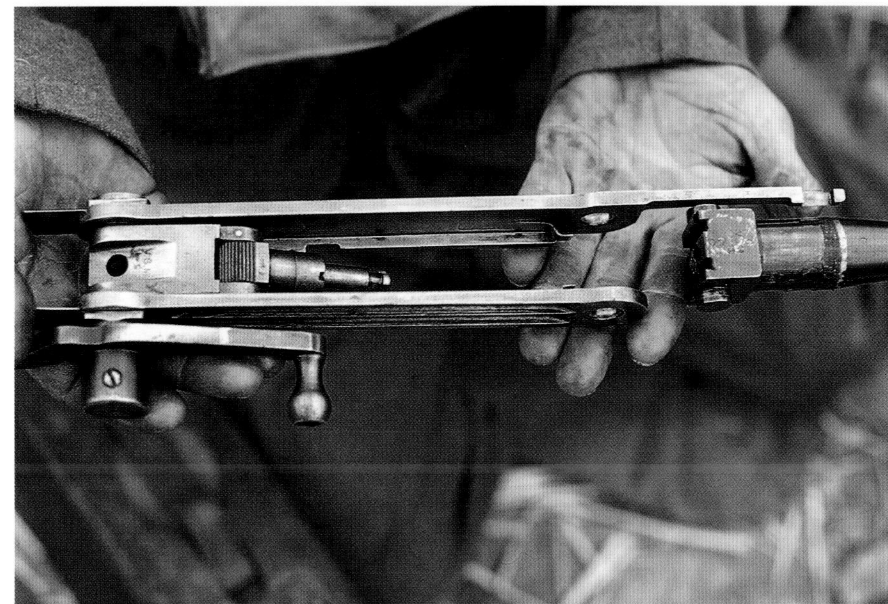

Detail of the "recoiling parts". Note how holes in the side plates engage with lugs on the barrel extension. The dull line around the barrel extension level with the gunner's left thumb is the asbestos string packing wound around it - correctly done, this seals water in the jacket while allowing free recoil of the barrel.

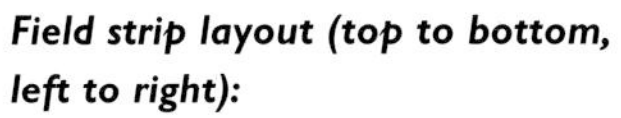

Field strip layout (top to bottom, left to right):
Receiver, T-bolt for backplate, barrel, fusee spring assembly, rear body pieces, lock assembly, feed block, muzzle cup, outer casing and cone, fusee chain, left side plate, muzzle cup spanner, .455in Webley revolver (standard issue to crew Nos. I and 2), crank handle assembly with right side plate, steam condensing hose (with postwar right-angled attachment), 250-round belt. The standard for an experienced gunner to strip and reassemble the Vickers was an astonishing 72 seconds.

Capt.Charles D.Chandler mans a prototype Lewis gun in a Wright Type B "pusher" biplane. This posed photo, showing Lt.Roy Kirkland at the controls, was taken soon after Chandler and the actual pilot, Lt.Milling, made aviation history by firing a machine gun from an aeroplane in flight for the first time on 7 June 1912. (NARA)

The Lewis, suitably modified, was very widely used in Allied aircraft; it was unsuitable for synchronised fire through the propellor, so was mounted either above the wing or - as on this de Havilland DH4B "trench strafer" - on Scarff ring mountings in the rear cockpit of two-seaters. These twin guns have 97-round pans, spade grips and muzzle boosters. For aerial use the redundant barrel cooling fins and shroud were removed. (NARA)

LEWIS Mk I

"After the enemy had also retired a little, an obstinate shooting match began. In the course of it a Lewis gun, posted fifty meters from us, forced us to duck our heads. A light machine gun on our side took the duel on. For half a minute the two murderous weapons rattled on at each other, with the bullets spurting round them. Then our gunner, the volunteer Motullo, was struck by a shot through the head. Though his brain fell over his face to his chin, his mind was still clear when we took him to the nearest dugout." (Ernst Junger, Leutnant, 73rd Hanoverian Fusilier Regiment, *The Storm of Steel*, 1929)

"The enemy fought with high courage, and there were many bombing duels, in which one of our sergeants caught German bombs before they burst and flung them back again - which is not an easy trick to learn. A Lewis gun was thrust up very quickly to a German post where a machine gun was concealed in a shell-crater, and played its hose on the team. . . . Out of one such strongpoint - a nest of craters - fifty-four Prussians came up with the usual shout of surrender." (Philip Gibbs, *The Battles of the Somme*, 1917)

Although several automatic rifles or light machine guns had been successfully fielded in the period leading up to the outbreak of war in 1914, only one was to prove itself entirely worthy of the men who trusted their lives to it amid the horrors of the Western Front. As with the Maxim gun, the Lewis was originally an American invention. At first spurned by its home country, it was enthusiastically received in Europe, appearing on the battlefields of the Western Front as the Model 1913 (Armes Automatiques Lewis, Liege, Belgium) and the Model 1914 (Birmingham Small Arms, UK). Turned out by the tens of thousands during the war - six could be made in the time and for the cost required by one Vickers/Maxim - it was far superior to its counterparts, the German MG08/15 and French Chauchat. The Lewis was the right weapon at the right time, and had a progressive effect on infantry tactics.

Development

The story of this remarkable weapon - properly called a "light automatic machine rifle" - began in 1910, when an American named Samuel McClean assigned all his mechanical patent rights to the Automatic Arms Co. of Buffalo, New York. Among his many inventions was a machine gun so overburdened with gadgets that it was unsuitable for any purpose other than arousing mechanical curiosity. The US Army rejected it after a brief examination; and the company scrambled about for some way to save their considerable investment. They were fortunate in persuading US Army Col.Isaac Newton Lewis to undertake the formidable task of reworking the McClean system into a feasible weapon.

This gifted engineer and inventor wisely retained McClean's basic (and safely patented) operating system, consisting of a gas piston acting on a camming slot in the bolt to rotate it for locking and unlocking. Lewis added the clock-type return spring, pan magazine and finned air-cooled barrel jacket. By 1911 he was able to conduct a number of live fire demonstrations of prototypes before various dignitaries and the US Army General Staff at Fort Myer, Virginia. These aroused considerable interest, and a formal trial was scheduled by the Army's Board of Ordnance and Fortifications for summer 1912.

General view of the Lewis Mk I (left to right, top to bottom:) gun, spare parts tin, barrel wrench, oil can, tool roll, anti-aircraft front sight, 97-round aircraft drum for comparison, helmet with sandbag cover, underside of 47-round drum, pouch, loading tool, optional "spade grip", Webley revolver as issued to Lewis gunners.

Reconstruction - Western Front, 1917: Behind the forward trenches, a lightly equipped Lewis gun No.1 and a member of his section move along a communication trench. At 33lbs (14.9kg) complete with a 47-round magazine the Lewis was a manageable slung load for a reasonably fit man. The "ammunition number" wears four circular webbing pouches each accomodating two Lewis drums; the full combat load for Nos.6, 7 and 8 in the section was four pouches plus another four magazines in a canvas bucket-shaped carrier - 12 drums, or 564 rounds each.

Preparing to go briefly "over the top" to reach his assigned fire position; not only was the Lewis ten pounds lighter than the German equivalent 08/15, but its compact and balanced design made it much easier to handle. Note the wreathed "LG" skill-at-arms badge above his rank chevron, introduced in 1917 for qualified Lewis gunners. Immediately left of his thumb underneath the barrel shroud note the protruding gas regulator.

One of the Lewis gunners' missions, as defined by official doctrine, was to move out under cover of a short local artillery barrage to take up positions forward of the main trench line. There they would hunt and kill German machine gun teams, snipers or other targets of opportunity; the Lewis gun's design allowed it to be fired without exposing the gunner to enemy fire any more than a rifleman. Here the No.2 is armed with the standard Short Magazine Lee Enfield .303in rifle, complete with wire-cutter muzzle fitting; this guides a strand of wire directly in front of the muzzle to be cut by a bullet.

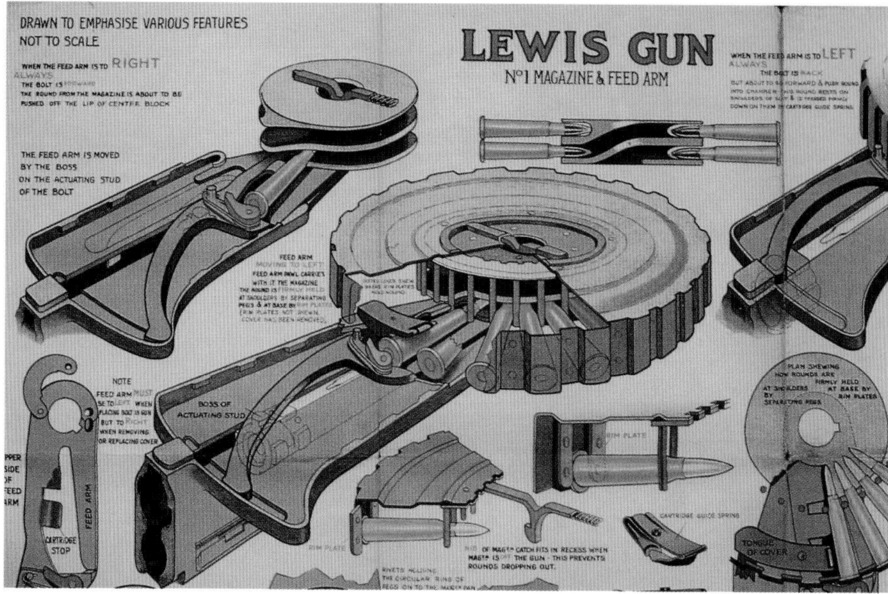

Detail, from one of Handley-Read's superb coloured instructional diagrams, showing the feed action as cartridges are indexed in the magazine for feeding and chambering. The actuating stud atop the bolt moves the feed arm with each round fired. (USAMHI)

BELOW *The No.2, normally burdened with the spares parts bag, carried only a pair of two-drum pouches (188 rounds). No.3, with two pouches, also acted as an ammo courier between the gun and the rest of the section; riflemen Nos.4 and 5 were scouts.*

The next step of this visionary inventor and promoter was to arrange an event that would excite imaginations all around the world. On 7 June 1912, with a prototype Lewis gun resting on the foot bar of a Wright Type B biplane flown by Lt.T.DeWitt Milling, Capt.Charles DeForest Chandler, commander of the US Army airfield at College Park, Maryland, became the first man in history to fire a machine gun while in flight. A posed photograph taken by an amateur was picked up and printed by newspapers and magazines worldwide as yet another amazing milestone in the new age of invention.

Unfortunately for Col.Lewis, the Automatic Arms Co. and the American soldier, the US Army high command curtly dismissed the whole episode, asserting that aircraft were only suitable for scouting and could never serve as platforms for aerial gunnery. The Ordnance Board test that immediately followed Chandler's history-making flight was no more positive. Perhaps due to the severity of the tests or even to actual faults in the prototype guns, the Lewis was neither accepted nor rejected. According to David Truby in his excellent book *The Lewis Gun*, the disappointed Lewis bitterly denounced the Ordnance establishment as "ignorant hacks." Rather than continue what seemed to be an exercise in futility in the face of hidebound prejudice, Col.Lewis turned in his retirement papers and steamed for Belgium in January 1913. Carefully crated in the hold were four of the 30.06 calibre guns which had been hand made for the US Army trials.

His reception in Europe was more gratifying; and after a series of demonstrations Belgium decided to adopt the gun in British .303in calibre, to be manufactured at Liege by the newly formed Armes Automatiques Lewis. Soon afterwards the respected British firm of Birmingham Small Arms (BSA) was granted a license; and the Lewis was in full production at both factories by June 1914. By 1916 more than 50,000 had been turned out in Belgium, Britain, and in America by the Savage Arms Company.

Trial by fire

The performance of the new Lewis gun quickly overshadowed that of the Benet-Mercié machine rifle, the only other light automatic in widespread use. Being the

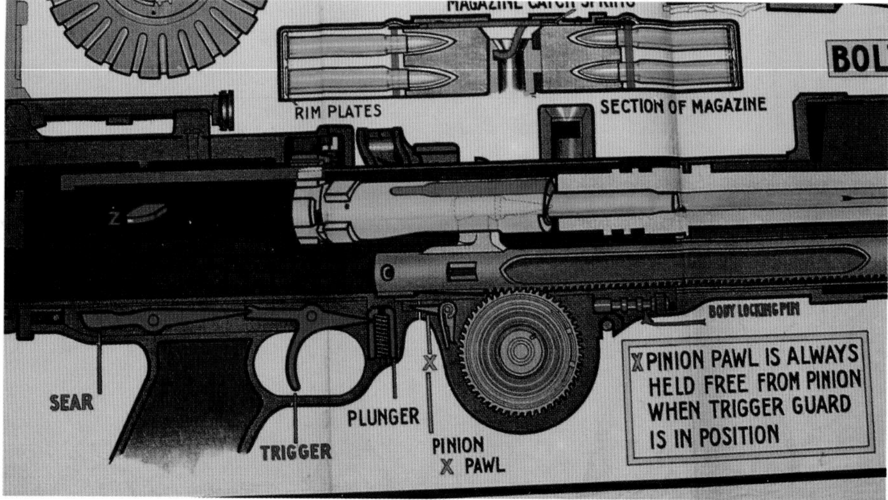

RIGHT *Detail by Handley-Read of the bolt and operating rod system an instant after firing. Propellant gas will enter the cylinder (here, green) near the muzzle to kick the piston end of the operating rod. After a momentary "dwell" as the operating rod moves backward and chamber pressure drops, the bolt will be turned to unlock as it moves back in the receiver. The clockwork spring in the gear housing (ahead of the trigger guard) is wound tighter as the operating rod/bolt carrier moves rearward, while the expended cartridge case is extracted and ejected.* (USAMHI)

first truly successful type of its kind in a period of rapid invention naturally meant that the Lewis would be linked with a number of innovations in the science of warfare.

Modified Lewis guns in single or double overwing mountings would become standard equipment for British scout aircraft and, on pivoting Scarff ring mounts, for the observers of two-seaters. The first night fighters mounting Lewis guns equipped with yellow phosphorous incendiary ammo would destroy the hydrogen-filled German Zeppelin dirigibles which bombed English cities. The Royal Navy took Lewis guns aboard ship to be used by boarding parties, for deck protection and against hostile aircraft. The British Army fitted them to armoured cars, tanks and motorcycles; and a special monopod adaptor was issued for quick mounting on posts or stumps for anti-aircraft defence. Indeed, wherever the tactical situation called for a fast-handling, fast-firing gun the Lewis was to be found.

Despite all these specialist applications, however, the Lewis's most significant contribution to the British Army's war-winning capability was in providing the rifle platoon with its own immediately available automatic support fire, and thus making the platoon the group around which new and more flexible "minor tactics" could develop. In 1915 the first issue was on a scale of only three per battalion. By the Battle of the Somme in mid-1916 each platoon had one Lewis, served by a section of eight men under a junior NCO and carrying 44 magazines - over 2,000 rounds of ammunition. The scale of issue increased during 1917, and 36 per battalion would become standard in 1918 - two per platoon, plus four in the anti-aircraft role with battalion headquarters.

As mentioned in the chapters on the MG08/15 and Vickers, the new ability of infantry platoons to carry their own automatic weapons into any tactical situation where a rifleman could go transformed infantry tactics forever. This new relationship between a machine gun team and a rifle-and-grenade team, working in concert by fire and movement, was born in 1916 - and born of the availability of the Lewis gun, which by the climactic battles of 1918 represented the infantry's main firepower.

The gun was so well regarded and so prominent in combat that contemporary newspaper accounts often singled it out for favourable comment. One such story, filed by British correspondent Sidney Brooks, appeared in the *Philadelphia Public Ledger* on 14 February 1917 (repeated in Vol.1 of Col.George M.Chinn's classic *The Machine Gun*):

"The present war is so largely a war of machine guns - I remember [Prime Minister] Lloyd George stating that more than ninety percent of the casualties were due to them alone - that whereas, at its beginning, we had only two guns to each thousand men, we now have thirty-two. Second, that of all the machine guns in use in the Allied armies, the Lewis is the most popular and the most effective by far.

A special tool engages the indexing notch in the central hub of the magazine, and turns it as each round is placed nose-first between the locating pegs and into the hub's spiral track. In operation, the central hub remains stationary while the cartridge-filled pan rotates. With no springs to apply excessive tension when new or to weaken with repeated use, there is no need to short-load the 47-round magazine. Note how the base of each cartridge is held neatly in a notch in the magazine rim.

Although the pans were easily filled by hand, this tool was useful when armourers needed to fill large numbers at speed. From the Hand-Book of the Lewis Machine Gun Model 1917, *Savage Arms Co. (Author's collection)*

BELOW LEFT *The tapered extension of the barrel shroud serves both as an efficient flash hider, and to stimulate airflow along the barrel. Its clamping ring incorporates the foresight. The bipod, well located near the muzzle, has telescoping legs independently adjustable by wing nuts. The fold-up "feet", to prevent the legs sinking into soft ground, are a neat idea but ineffective in the kind of mud found on the Western Front.*

Under the shroud the gas regulator protrudes ahead of the bipod, its key through and behind it; the key engages with the regulator to lock it in position with the selected size of hole lined up between the barrel gas take-off and the gas cylinder.

BELOW *The spring scale is used to gauge the amount of tension exerted by the clockwork recoil spring on the operating rod. Too much tension causes excessively fast firing, with a risk of breakage of parts: too little, and the gun won't feed and lock properly.*

The left side of the receiver, showing the rear end of the aluminium heat-dissipating fins at the chamber area. The rear sight is folded down for protection while carrying. The cut-out at the top front of the buttstock comfortably accomodates the gunner's left hand for steadiness while firing. The pistol grip is well configured to the hand and its angle is best for prone shooting. NB: the "stirrup" handle pivoting at the rear of the barrel shroud in all these photos is in fact a post-Great War item and would not have been seen on the Western Front.

A detail from the US 1917 manual for the .30-06 Lewis illustrates how the barrel shroud extension (3-4) and barrel mouthpiece (3-2) produce a vacuum through overpressure when each round is fired, drawing a cooling flow of air through the shroud from the receiver end. Note also the adjustable gas regulator system (3-5 to 3-8). (Author's collection)

Third. . .that in the British, French, Italian and Russian armies there are at this moment nearly 40,000 in actual and daily operation. Fourth, that virtually all our aeroplanes are armed with the Lewis guns and that of the seven Zeppelins we have accounted for, six were brought down by the Lewis gun. Fifth, that it owes its pre-eminence partly to its mobility, partly to its light weight, partly to its capability of being used in any position and partly to the simplicity of its workings; and that after fully two years of daily service on the battlefield, it stands higher than ever in the judgement of the British armies."

Characteristics:

Feed and cooling

One of the most distinctive and desirable aspects of the Lewis is its top-mounted "pan"-type magazine, a refinement of the impractically large Carr drum. Colonel Lewis reduced it to a light and handy 47-round drum for ground use; with no springs to break or weaken with use, and no bothersome belt to drag along, the Lewis magazine offered significant advantages over competing designs.

Less immediately obvious but equally important is the efficient cooling provided by the barrel shroud extension. Quite unlike modern squad automatic weapons with their slotted flash suppressors, the "totally tubular" Lewis shoots the muzzle blast forward along with the bullets. The tapered end of the barrel shroud is a separate piece, clamped in place by a metal band which also incorporates the front sight. (This extension serves not only to siphon cool air over the radiator fins along the barrel, but also as a very efficient flash hider; it significantly reduces the enemy's ability to locate the gun at any angle other than head-on when firing at night.)

With its stovepipe-like shape, this prominent barrel shroud invites explanation. One might reasonably think that an air-cooled weapon would benefit most from unimpeded natural airflow over the steel barrel and its full length aluminium radiator fins. However, Col.Lewis specifically designed it to draw cooling air from the receiver end through the shroud as the gun is fired. This is accomplished by the

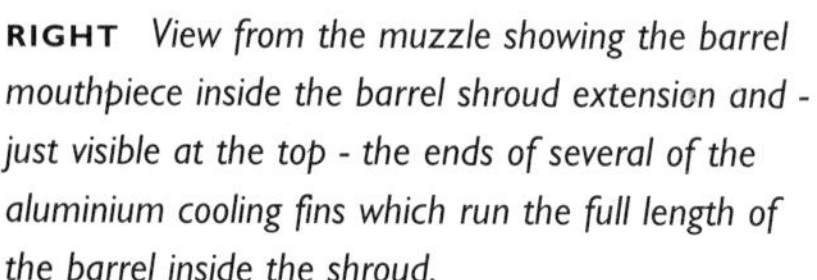

RIGHT *View from the muzzle showing the barrel mouthpiece inside the barrel shroud extension and - just visible at the top - the ends of several of the aluminium cooling fins which run the full length of the barrel inside the shroud.*

FAR RIGHT *The very precise, if somewhat fragile aperture rear sight is adjusted with micrometer precision by turning the elevating knob at the top; the scale is marked in 100-yard increments from 400 to 2,100 yards.*

tapered extension at the muzzle end: blast overpressure causes a vacuum, and stimulates airflow with each cartridge fired. His novel method apparently worked well enough; with the obvious exception of aircraft guns, the shroud and fin system was retained in all the various models made and used during the Great War.

A set of anti-aircraft sights are part of each gun's kit, consisting of a clamp-on ring foresight with an elliptical design for judging "lead", and a smaller brass aperture which attaches to the rear sight ladder. Note the substitution here of a 97-round magazine, and a rear "spade grip" in place of the buttstock.

Cycle of operation

(As described in Chinn's *The Machine Gun, Vol.1*:)

"Locking of the breech depends on the semi-circular movement of locking lugs at the rear of the rotating bolt, a principle first used by the Mannlicher and Schmidt-Rubin rifles. The striker (firing pin) is located on a post fixed at the rear of the gas piston rod assembly and rides back and forth in a slot cut in the body of the bolt.

"When the piston is engaged by the sear, the bolt is held retracted in the open position. When the trigger is pulled, the piston and bolt are driven forward by the clock-type return spring, while the face of the bolt pushes the already indexed cartridge ahead of it into the chamber.

"At this point the striker post is held securely in a recess at the rear of the bolt slot, with its left side bearing against an inner portion of the curved part of the bolt slot. The locking lugs on the bolt engage with the guide grooves on the receiver and prevent the bolt from being rotated until the lugs are opposite their locking recesses. The continued forward motion of the striker post along the curved portion of its slot rotates the bolt body and lugs in their recesses, while the striker continues along a straight path in the slot until its point smashes into the primer to fire the chambered cartridge.

"The barrel, bolt and piston are all securely locked until the bullet has passed an orifice in the barrel at which gas is allowed into a cylinder and it kicks back against the gas piston. By the time the action begins a rearward motion, the bullet has safely cleared the muzzle and the gas piston is then suddenly thrust back with great pressure.

"The movement of the piston assembly withdraws the striker and the rotation of the bolt caused by the striker post in the camming slot unlocks the action. The extractor withdraws the cartridge case as the bolt rides back and a pivoting ejector knocks the case out of the ejection port. The continued rearward action of the gas piston assembly also actuates the . . .drum magazine rotation lug, causing it to move a precise fraction of a revolution to index the incoming round to be picked up by the bolt once again."

(This highly successful mechanism would be revived by the Germans in WWII in their FG42 paratrooper's machine rifle, and in America in time for the Vietnam War in the M60 machine gun; see *German Automatic Weapons of World War II* in this book series.)

USA, 1917: this straining Doughboy was presumably ordered to demonstrate standing shoulder fire for an official photo. The front-heavy balance of the gun, weighing 33lbs with a loaded pan, made this impractical in actual combat. (NARA)

Drawbacks

While the Lewis was certainly superior to its counterparts both on the ground and in the air, this is not to imply that it was perfect in every way. As with any innovative weapon, it did have drawbacks which contributed to problems under battlefield conditions.

Despite the cooling fins the barrel would overheat in sustained fire, with a resultant loss of accuracy and barrel life. The clock-type return spring tended to become brittle from repeated overheating and, perversely but inevitably, would always break at the worst possible moment. The magazines were sometimes tem-

The blade front sight, mounted on the shroud extension clamping ring, is protected by a pair of vertical "wings"; unusually, it can be adjusted for windage to zero the weapon.

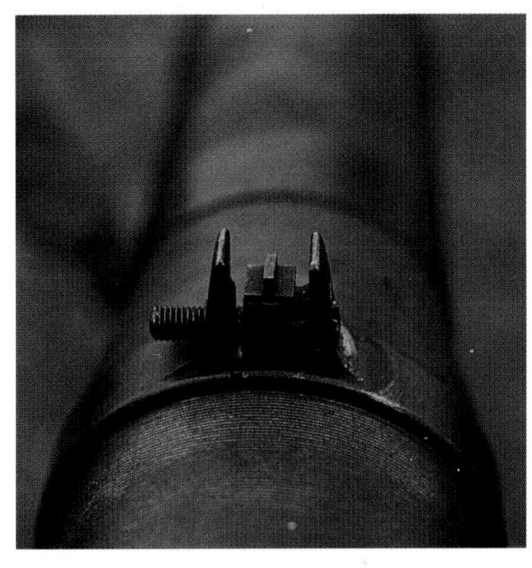

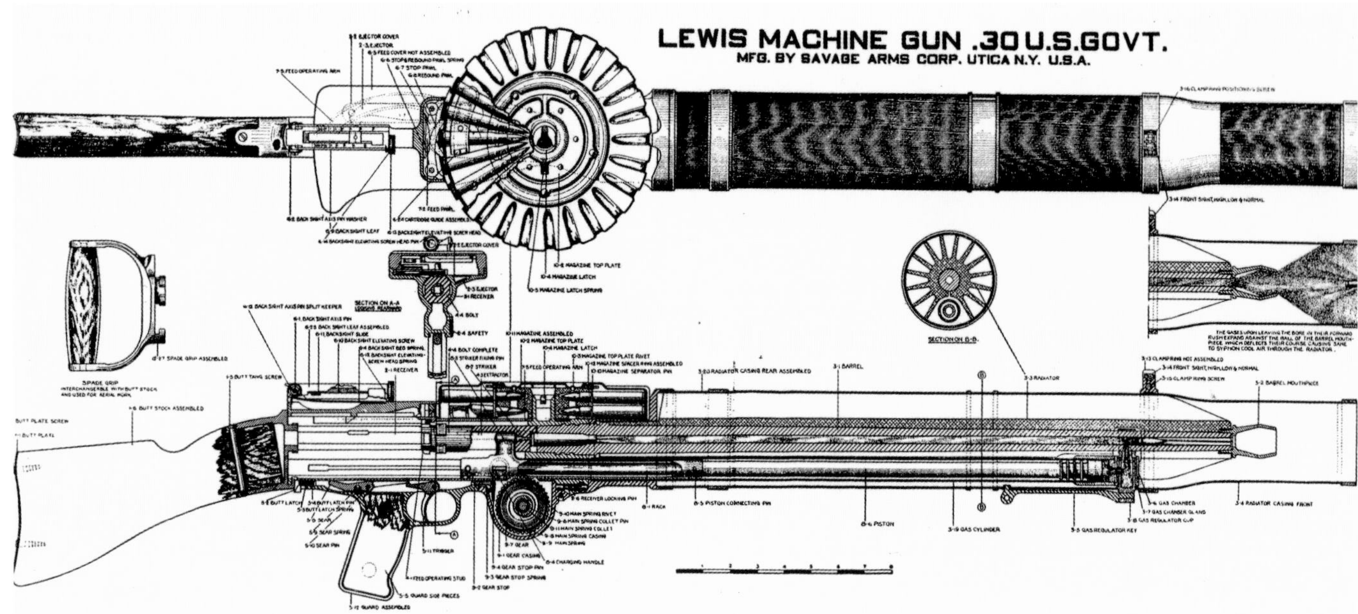

Excellent line drawing with cutaway views of the .30-06 American Lewis, a fold-out in the information and sales brochure published by Savage Arms Co. (Author's collection)

peramental, and always liable to jamming caused by rough handling or battlefield dirt - their open bottom surface was naturally vulnerable. The totally enclosed receiver, while resistant to entry of dirt and moisture, made it difficult to clear a jammed cartridge case quickly in either the feed or extraction phases.

The "Belgian Rattlesnake" and US Lewis

The Germans were not slow to note the implications of the light, portable machine rifle, and their troops bitterly dubbed the Lewis the "Belgian Rattlesnake". As already described, in response to the same tactical problems which the Lewis solved for the British, they lightened their Maxim MG08 to produce the 08/15 - much heavier and more unwieldy than the Lewis, and never more than an unsatisfactory compromise, though tactically significant nonetheless. The German Army were quick to exploit every Lewis they could capture, and included its care and operation as an integral part of the instruction of all new machine gunners.

American soldiers had first used .303in Lewis guns on the Mexican border in 1916. Bowing to public pressure built upon more than two years of combat success in Europe, Col.Lewis's own army finally adopted the .30-06 calibre Lewis Machine Gun Model 1917, manufactured by Savage Arms Co. of Utica, New York. However, the US Army still wasn't too fond of these guns due to early teething problems caused by dimensional changes and the substantially more powerful US cartridge. An improved version, the Model 1918, was widely used by the US Marines and Navy, and the calibre .30 Lewis Aircraft Machine Gun Model 1918 was completely successful in use by the US Army's flyers.

Soldiers of the US 29th Infantry Division training at Ft.McClellan, Alabama, in 1917 before being shipped out to France with Pershing's AEF. Slow to adopt the Lewis despite its glowing record in British use, the US Army finally began to procure .30-06 cal. guns from the Savage Arms Co. in 1917. (NARA)

Lewis Mk I Technical Specifications

Nomenclature	Gun, Machine, Lewis 0.303in Mark I
Manufacturer	Birmingham Small Arms Co., England
Calibre	.303in (7.62mm)
Ammunition	Mk VII ball; armour piercing; tracer; incendiary; blank
System of operation	Gas, open bolt
Cooling	Air; aluminium radiator-finned barrel
Selector	None; full automatic only
Feed	47-round horizontal top-mounted drum magazine
Length	50.5ins (1282.7mm)
Barrel	26.04ins (670.5mm); 4 grooves, left twist
Weight, gun	28.25lbs (12.8kg) w/bipod, unloaded
Weight, loaded mag	4.5lbs (2.04kg)
Mount	Detachable bipod; adaptable to Vickers tripod
Sights	Blade front; aperture rear on leaf
Rate of fire	500-600rpm
Muzzle velocity	2,450fps (745mps)
Max.range	1,900 yards
Max.effective range	Approx.800-1,000 yards

ABOVE LEFT *Note the spline on the magazine post, aligning with the notch in the hub of the pan. The weight of the filled magazine drops it into place on the post and a tab on the top locks it in place. During firing, cartridges spiral down the track in the stationary central hub as the rest of the magazine turns.*

ABOVE RIGHT *The gun is cocked by pulling the cocking ("charging") handle all the way to the rear, where it locks the bolt in place. This handle can be positioned optionally on either the left or the right side of the bolt. The long horizontal strip of steel below its track on either side of the receiver serves as the safety catch. The handle is pulled back, and the safety strip is pushed upwards using the horizontal protrusion above the trigger as a thumbpiece; a notch at the upper rear of the strip locks the shaft of the cocking handle.*

Firing the Lewis

The gun kindly provided by Great War enthusiast Mike Knapp, a BSA-made Mk I, was a flawless performer. It ingested and fired more than 600 rounds of British 1940s-production .303 ammunition without skipping a beat, and without requiring adjustment of the clock spring (12lbs) or the gas port (No.1 setting). We fired in various positions from prone to walking hip-fire, and at one stage ran through a full 47-round pan with one long squeeze of the trigger.

Had we encountered problems with Knapp's gun, a quick consultation of any of the editions of the official *Handbook of the Lewis Gun* would have set us straight. All contain tables and illustrations showing how to identify stoppages by any of three main positions of the cocking handle, and how to remedy their probable causes.

The furthest extent of range safely allowed by the terrain and surrounding farmhouses was some 150 yards. We set up one half and one full silhouette to represent a pair of human targets. Starting from a prone, bipod-supported position Knapp ripped into them, firing short bursts into first one and then the other; at such a short but realistic battle range the accuracy was impressive. With the pictures I needed "in the can", it was my turn to test fire the Lewis and record my impressions.

Assault firing

The first is that the gun is very front-heavy. Despite good placement of the magazine, little can be done to overcome all that steel and aluminium hanging around 26ins (660mm) of barrel when firing from anything above the prone position. This is partially overcome in walking assault fire by hanging the comfortably wide and correctly attached sling over one's shoulder. Even so, some care must be taken to keep the rotating pan magazine from too much contact with uniform or web gear; this necessitates pushing the whole thing forward again, which rather defeats the effect of the sling and can quickly get tiring.

Some definite pluses in this firing position are the very mild recoil despite the full-powered rifle cartridges, and the lack of sonic assault on unprotected ears. The first is attributable to the weight of the gun, and the second to the super-efficient flash hider/barrel shroud extension.

The barrel shroud's finely checkered surface is interesting. Although it is presumably intended to provide a no-slip surface, it is a foolish gunner who grasps it with a bare hand anywhere near the chamber area after rapid fire of a couple of pans. The slip-ring mounted "stirrup" carrying handle shown in our photos, and much appreciated during our assault fire tests, is in fact a post-Great War accessory; during the war the only aid apart from the sling was a fabric carrying handle in this position devised by some unit saddlers for troops in the Middle East theatre.

Westfront, 1917: a German motorcyclist roars up a hill with a captured Lewis slung over his back - the light and powerful "Belgian rattlesnake" was coveted as distinctly superior to the water-cooled MG08/15. (NARA)

Prone firing

Despite the theoretical value of "walking fire", better and more tactically sound results are obtained when shooting from the lowest possible profile - prone, bipod-supported fire gives minimal exposure with maximal accuracy.

The Lewis **bipod** functions well in medium to long range shooting, being rigidly mounted near the muzzle - a good compromise, facilitating both accuracy and quick traverse. Sturdily made in the piston-and-sleeve style, each leg can be independently extended to level the gun on uneven terrain. Most models have

The gunner pulls the buttstock firmly into the pocket of his shoulder, and aligns the exceptionally well positioned sights.

spike-bottomed legs for a stable grip, combined with little flip-up "feet" to keep the legs from sinking into soft earth (a nice thought, but these don't work worth a damn in soft mud).

The ergonomic accomodation of man to machine in the Lewis gun is very good; much thought has gone into the angle and shape of both the **buttstock** and the **pistol grip**. One small criticism is the lack of a flip-up shoulder rest on the buttplate. This seemingly insignificant provision would allow the gunner to rest his arm muscles between bursts instead of maintaining rigid tension at all times to keep the sights on the target area; an exhausted or even a wounded gunner can still continue to fire effectively when aided by a shoulder rest.

Among the tools commonly included in the leather gunner's roll are spring scales, spare bolt, spanners and broken case extractor.

The correct position for firing most automatic rifles is with the body in as straight a line as possible to the axis of recoil. Lie on your belly directly behind the gun, and place the buttstock in the "pocket" of the shoulder. The right hand grasps the pistol grip and pulls the stock firmly against the shoulder. The left elbow is placed in contact with the ground, and the left hand is used to steady the buttstock. Interestingly, according to British manuals the left hand is placed over the buttstock in the specially shaped cut where it joins the receiver; but in American manuals the left hand is placed under the toe of the stock, thereby helping to hold everything up.

The design and placement of the **rear sight** are exactly right. Folded down for protection when carrying, it snaps instantly and securely upright. It isn't too close to interfere with the brim of a steel helmet, and its aperture is suspended at just the right height and distance for highly accurate shooting with no neck strain. It is adjustable in 100-yard increments between 400 and 2,100 yards.

The **front sight** is a blade protected by vertical "wings", mounted on the clamping band for the barrel shroud extension; it is adjustable for windage by means of a screw in its base. While entirely impractical in combat, this provision allows the gun to be precisely "zeroed" on the range. In action, the gunner adjusts fire by observing the strike of a burst and then "holds off" to one side or another as necessary. The Lewis's exceptional 32in (812mm) sight radius - the distance between front and rear sights - also contributes to pinpoint accuracy at greater than normal distances.

Anyone who has fired more than a few rounds from a full-powered military bolt action rifle knows that **recoil** or "kick" is a significant factor. This is particularly true in the prone position, where all the energy is caught in the shoulder and transmitted in shock waves through the whole body. Recoil is not a major concern to the Lewis gunner, however. This is due partly to its weight - three times that of the British SMLE infantry rifle - and partly to the ground-grabbing bipod, which helps hold the gun in place. A significant amount of recoil energy is also taken up in the cycling of the action, operated by propellant gas captured near the muzzle.

However, there is no such thing as a free lunch: the same cycling of parts serves to impair accuracy. The Lewis fires from an "open bolt" position, and there is appreciable movement of the gun when the trigger is released and the bolt and operating rod assembly slam forward to fire the first round. Again, "little recoil" doesn't mean "no recoil". The Lewis has to be held firmly when firing or dispersion becomes excessive. Gunner fatigue is also a factor after a few hundred rounds of rapid shoulder-thumping. There is a reason why Lewis gunners were supposed to be chosen only from among the largest and fittest men - and why modern squad automatic weapons, like modern rifles, are usually chambered for smaller cartridges and consequently weigh much less.

The Lewis has no selective fire capability, and is fired fully automatic at all times. Manuals talk of the ability to snap off single shots by pulling and quickly releasing the trigger, but in most tactical situations I believe this to be futile - better to squeeze off a short burst with its attendant higher hit probability than to waste effort trying to shoot the Lewis like a rifle. *(An experienced gunner's ability to squeeze off single shots was not wholly pointless, however. The late father of the editor of this book, Sgt.William Windrow of the London Scottish Regiment, was a Lewis instructor in 1917; in old age he spoke fondly of the amount of beer money he won off trainees by betting on this particular skill. Ed.)*

The gunner methodically searches his target with a series of short bursts of five or six rounds, checking his aim after each burst. The Lewis kicks up dirt in front with the shock wave at the muzzle; hot empties flip out of the ejection port to the right and forward of the gun onto the sandbags. Every other member of the section was trained to drop his rifle and take over as gun No.1 if need be.

Changing magazines

The handy location of the magazine in a horizontal plane on top of the receiver is superior to the arrangement of many contemporary and later weapons. The magazine does not scrape the ground underneath, or pull the weapon off balance by sticking out on one side or the other. Its low profile does not interfere with the sights, and it does not stick up like a lethal position marker above the gunner's head. In short, it seems to be ideal - except for the fact that it is, by necessity, completely open underneath. Still, the ammunition inside and the feed area of the gun are largely protected against the crippling ingestion of dirt and moisture - certainly much better so than in any belt-feed system.

Holding only 47 rounds, the magazine is quickly exhausted in action and must be changed frequently. Fortunately this is much more easily accomplished than with belt-fed guns, and nearly as easily as with a conventional modern box magazine. Grasp the magazine so that the thumb is able to feel the latch inside the central well, and lift free. Drop the new pan, with slot and spline aligned, onto the magazine post, turning it slightly in each direction to be sure it is seated and locked in place.

Unloading a partially expended magazine is trickier because a cartridge remains in the feedway. The easiest way to get rid of it is to pull the trigger

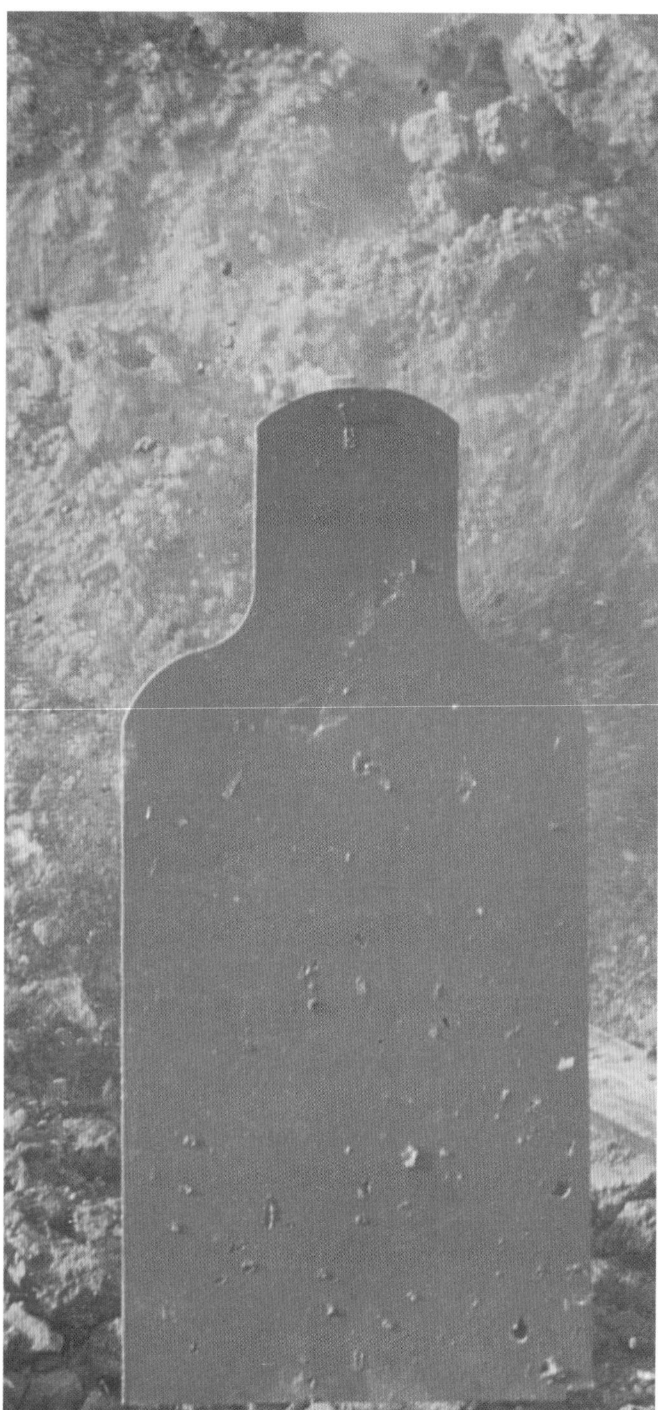

About 150 yards away over on the German side of the trench complex, a full sized "E" type cardboard silhouette is thoroughly ventilated by burst after burst. Another, half-height target shows the lethal effects of close range assault fire from the hip. "Walking fire" is a practical proposition with the very accurate Lewis, whose weight absorbs most of the recoil, and whose broad sling gives quite good support.

and fire it. However, if necessary the following steps may be followed, *with care*. Hold the cocking handle with the left hand; press the trigger with the right hand, and ease the cocking handle forward with just enough force to push the cartridge from the feed slot into the receiver body. Pull the cocking handle all the way back until the bolt locks in place. Raise the safety until it captures the cocking handle. Turn the gun on its side and shake the cartridge out through the ejector port.

Conclusion

The Lewis's manageable weight, rifle-like configuration, compact magazine feed, efficient air-cooling, adjustable sights and bipod, and relative cheapness and ease of manufacture put into the hands of the infantry platoon for the first time a fully automatic weapon capable of delivering close support fire in the assault, and allowing the average infantry soldier to effectively engage enemy targets out to 1,000 yards. Its appearance in quantity heralded a fundamental advance in small unit infantry tactics, whose essential features have remained unchanged ever since.

Credits

Gun owner & gunner, Mike Knapp, Falls Church, VA; assistant gunner, Steve Altemus, Alexandria, VA; uniforms & equipment, Knapp & Altemus; location assistant, John Exley IV, Mechanicsville, VA; range, Great War Association, Shimpstown, PA. Primary research source: Truby, David, *The Lewis Gun*.

STRIPPING THE LEWIS

After removing the magazine and inspecting the feedway and chamber to ensure that no live cartridges are present, hold the charging handle; squeeze the trigger, and allow the bolt to ride forward.

Disassembly begins by using e.g. a cartridge to trip the buttstock latch, central under the rear of the receiver behind the pistol grip. Twist the buttstock anti-clockwise until it can be removed from the receiver.

Holding the trigger, slide the trigger housing group to the rear and clear of the receiver.

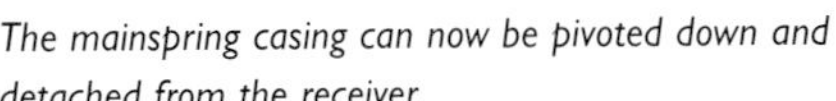

The mainspring casing can now be pivoted down and detached from the receiver.

LEFT *Pull the cocking handle all the way to the back of the receiver, where it can be withdrawn.*

CENTRE LEFT *The entire operating rod and bolt assembly can now be withdrawn through the back of the receiver.*

BOTTOM *Move the feed operating arm as far to the right as it will go, then push the feed cover toward the rear of the receiver until it separates. Note the profuse markings, including those of both the British manufacturers and the Belgian licensors, identification as a Model 1914, the serial 77651, the Army's broad arrow, and Birmingham proof marks.*

OPPOSITE TOP *Remove the feed arm assembly by unlatching it at the magazine post.*

OPPOSITE CENTRE LEFT *View of the major components of the feed system. The bolt has been put back into the gun - showing here bright silver in the central feedway - to show the stud protruding from its top rear, which moves the feed arm assembly as it reciprocates in the receiver during firing.*

OPPOSITE CENTRE RIGHT *Relationship of the main parts of the action. The bolt, top, is in the unlocked position on the operating rod; the striker post and firing pin mounted on the rod are hidden inside the curved slot in the bolt. As the rod runs forward under mainspring tension, transmitted by a gear and tooth system, the bolt pushes a cartridge from the feedway toward the chamber, and the forward movement of the striker post in the curved slot also rotates the bolt to lock its lugs.*

BOTTOM *While the barrel group can easily be removed from the receiver, this is not necessary for routine maintenance.*

Field strip layout (top to bottom, left to right):

Feed cover, feed arm assembly, barrel and receiver group, buttstock with sling attached (note asbestos liner to protect it when in contact with hot barrel shroud), cartridge, operating rod assembly, trigger housing group, charging handle, gear casing, pan magazine.

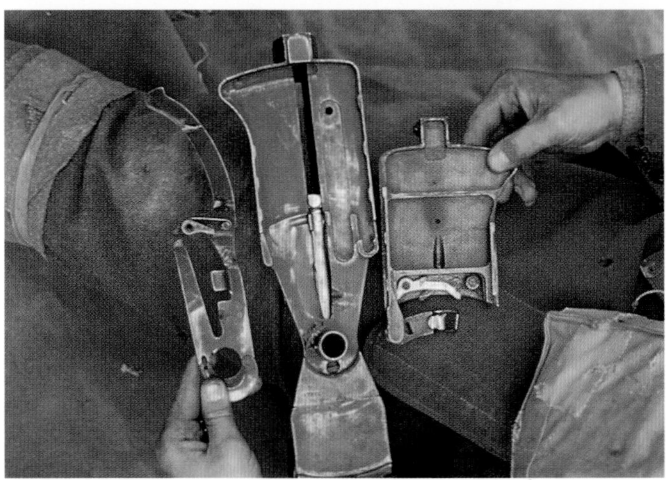

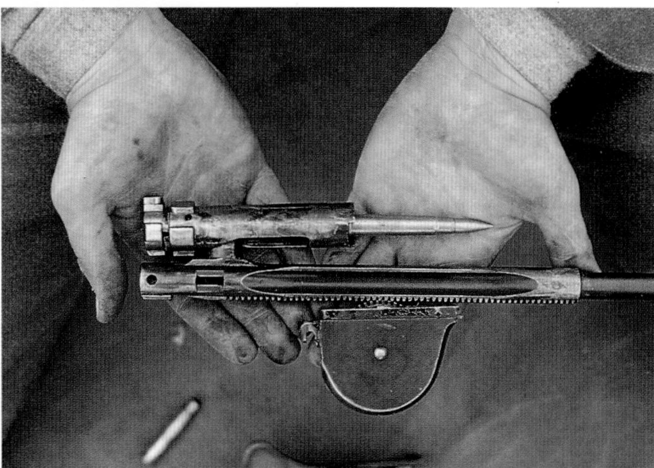

The elegant lines of the Mle 1914 Mitrailleuse Hotchkiss; although its air-cooled barrel and metal strip feed system set it apart from the Maxim designs used by most other armies, its simplicity and reliability made it a favourite with French and American soldiers. Note the wooden box for 12 feed strips; the spare barrel; and, particularly, the tripod. Rather than the Affut Mle 1915 Omnibus or more common Affut Mle 1916, this is a 360-degree traverse M1916 Hotchkiss Machine Gun Tripod made by Standard Parts Co. of Cleveland, Ohio. Wartime production at Hotchkiss could barely keep up with demand, and contracts were placed with American companies for mounts, spares and ammunition.

OPPOSITE TOP *Reconstruction - Western Front, 1918: An emergency signal flare arcs over No Man's Land, illuminating a Hotchkiss crew in a blood-red glow. These two poilus man the gun alone during their night watch in a second line trench while their comrades snatch what sleep they can in a nearby dugout. Their primary mission is to provide covering fire against German assaults and overhead fire for protection of wiring parties at night; secondary missions include indirect fire against known troop concentrations and harassing fire on communication trenches. They are wearing 1916 pattern leather gear over standard 1915 pattern "horizon blue" wool uniforms and Adrian helmets.*

OPPOSITE BOTTOM LEFT *Soldier of the 151eme RI lugging the 54lb (24kg) gun through the communication trenches; it balances reasonably well on the shoulder, but the standard padded leather shoulder protector would be appreciated.*

OPPOSITE BOTTOM RIGHT *A veteran gun commander checks the aim of his piece; note the finely machined steel of the receiver and the cast brass grip and trigger housing group. Receiver markings include the calibre - versions of the Hotchkiss were made in the rifle calibres of several foreign armies.*

HOTCHKISS Mle 1914

"And the machine gun is a coquette, too. Under its appearance of delicacy and grace it conceals a terrible power of domination and strength. . . .Fashioned like a work of art, the brilliancy of its polished steel and the voluptuous roundness of the brass invite caresses. Its shots come from they know not where, since they can see nothing - a bush is sufficient to conceal it; light, it is here one minute and there another; it is not visible until one is almost upon it, yet its shots are fatal at some miles. It is delicate and costly, needing a hundred things for its adornment, skilled care for its toilette and a hundred men to serve it - is not the machine gun a coquette?" (Sgt.Maj.Georges Lafond, French Colonial Infantry, *Covered with Mud and Glory*, 1918)

The air-cooled, strip-fed, gas-operated Hotchkiss machine gun boasts a distinguished record of service from the turn of the century until the 1950s. Designed by a captain in the Austrian Army and perfected by an American engineer working in France, this gun served faithfully in the Russo-Japanese War, World Wars I and II, in French Indochina, and in many other colonial and secondary conflicts. Cleverly configured to avoid patent infringement lawsuits, the Hotchkiss was the world's only truly successful air-cooled heavy machine gun before the appearance of the German MG34 in the 1930s.

Development

Hiram Maxim's first public demonstrations of his "automatic machine gun" in the 1880s aroused great excitement among European armies. Inventors in many countries strove to create equally successful designs; but the trick was to accomplish an equally good combination of feed, locking, operation and cooling without infringing the many patents held by Maxim. Laurence V. Benet, the American-born chief engineer of the Paris firm owned by fellow American Benjamin Hotchkiss, recalled in a spring 1937 article:

"The first gas-operated machine gun of which I have knowledge was brought to the attention of the Hotchkiss company in 1893 by an Austrian cavalry officer, Baron (Adolph von) Odkalek. His model gun was a very crude affair, capable of firing not more than a dozen or so rounds without a breakdown. However, the idea was there - and the possibility of developing an efficient weapon. His patents were acquired for a very considerable sum, and from them was developed the well-known Hotchkiss system of automatic arms."

It must have been quite a job for Benet and his French assistant Henri Mercié to bring the Odkalek gun up to speed, because serious live-fire testing did not begin until two years later. It soon became apparent that the problem of excessive heat would be a major stumbling block: if a gun works well enough to fire for long periods without breaking down, the barrel quickly overheats, loses accuracy and wears out prematurely. Maxim solved this by encasing his barrel in a patented water jacket; Benet had to come up with something different.

Hotchkiss factory publicity photo, c.1903, showing a Mle 1900 gun loaded with a 250-round "semi-articulated band" made up of three-round metal sections joined by hinge pins. Note the early tripod with seat, and the use of a shoulder stock. (NARA)

MITRAILLEUSE AUTOMATIQUE HOTCHKISS
BREVETEE S.G.D.G.
CALIBRE 8

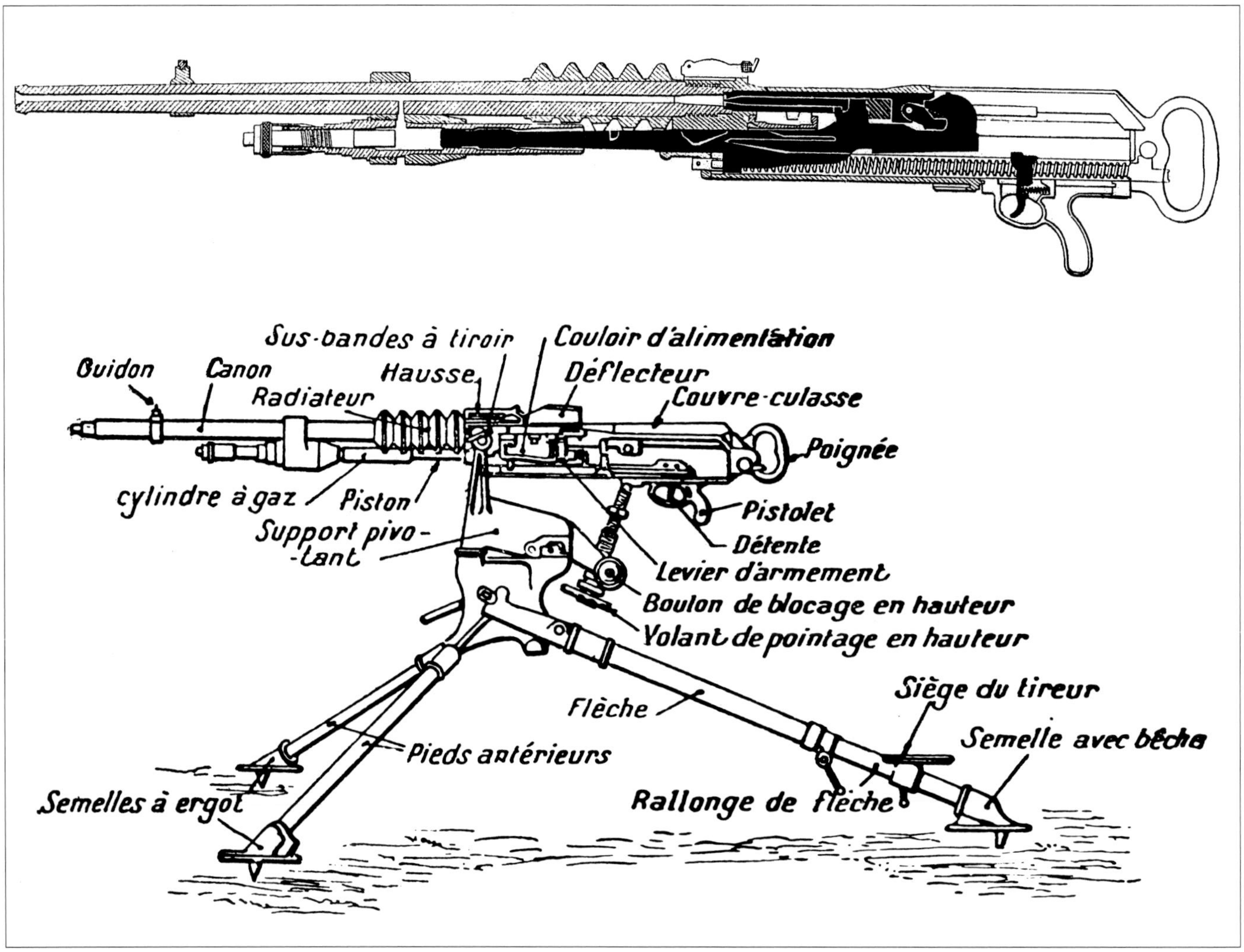

The main parts of the Hotchkiss Mle 1914 and the Mle 1916 tripod are named in this illustration from the 1917 Manuel de la Mitrailleuse Automatique Hotchkiss *(courtesy Gerard Demaison). The smaller cutaway diagram is from Capt.Robert's* ABC du Mitrailleur *of 1917. The moving parts shown in solid black include the bolt and carrier on the gas piston and operating rod, shown at the moment of locking and cartridge detonation. (Author's collection)*

Struck by the idea of wrapping the barrel in large bronze doughnut-shaped rings to provide sufficient radiating surface for air cooling, he applied for a patent - only to find that American inventor Norman Wiard had beaten him to it over 30 years earlier; but a satisfactory arrangement must have been worked out with Wiard or his estate, because the prominent radiator rings became a distinguishing characteristic of this first and future Hotchkiss machine guns.

The resulting Mitrailleuse Hotchkiss Modele 1897 was both a practical infantry weapon and sufficiently unlike the Maxim to be commercially viable - no small accomplishment. Instead of Maxim's short recoil system it employed propellant gas vented below the barrel to drive a piston and bolt carrier rearward to cycle the mechanism. Because cloth belt feed was also patented, Benet used flat metal feed strips. The action locked by means of a hinged piece between the bolt and carrier which tipped up and down by action of the piston running back and forth.

The French Army had considerable colonial commitments in North Africa and Indochina, and purchased the air-cooled Hotchkiss in small numbers for its convenience of use in hot regions where water was always a problem. Large scale production only began when the somewhat improved Mle 1900 was sold in quantity to Japan and employed against Russia in their war over Manchuria in 1904-05. Japan was also granted a license for domestic production of a modified Mle 1900 adapted for her 6.5mm rifle cartridge.

This Hotchkiss crew in wooded terrain are well prepared for action with a large stack of feed strips at the ready, although it is not recommended to expose ammunition to dirt like this. (USACMH)

Improved ammunition

In the words, once again, of Laurence Benet: "In the case of the French 8mm ammunition, the bottleneck cartridge, designed for the under-barrel magazine of the Lebel rifle, presented great difficulties in feeding; and the loosely seated primers had a disconcerting way of dropping out under the action of the ejector. A dropped primer would jam the mechanism and it was generally necessary to strip the gun for its removal. This difficulty was overcome by so forming the face of the breechblock (bolt) that it crimped the primer firmly in place when the breech was closed. In later fabrication the primers were, of course, firmly seated and crimped. The solid copper French bullet, of well known accuracy, is the least destructive of the barrel of any in service."

An improved cartridge for French rifles and machine guns was adopted in 1912 to correct this problem: the Cartouche Modèle 1886D(am), the suffix standing for *amorcage modifié*, "modified primer". Propelled by 47.9 grains of nitrocellulose powder, its aerodynamic, pointed, boat-tailed "Spitzer" bullet had a very flat trajectory and a remarkable maximum range of 4,300 meters. Almost mocking the significantly improved ballistics of the bullet, the original sharply tapering, broad-based, thick-rimmed cartridge case - so bothersome to machine gun designers - had to be retained because of the millions of rifles already in service which required it.

Hotchkiss feed strips normally had a capacity of 24 rounds, but some 30-rounders have been encountered. They were carried for protection in hinged wooden cases holding 12 strips for a total of 288 rounds and weighing 12 kilos. The less often seen *bande articulée* was a 250-round semi-articulated belt consisting of three-round sections of metal strip connected by hinge pins. It was normally wound on a spool held inside a large aluminium ammunition can which attached to the side of the gun.

US Ordnance Corps photo of the Mle 1914 gun on the Mle 1915 Omnibus mount, recognisable by its large elevation handwheel set in the vertical plane. (NARA)

The Great War

On the eve of World War I the French, alarmed by large scale purchase of Maxims by Germany, ordered mass production of a simplified and improved Hotchkiss Mle 1914, characterised by fabrication of the radiator rings from steel rather than bronze and the elimination of the mechanical safety device.

Despite not having a water jacket, the Mle 1914 still weighed in at over 53lbs (24kg) - 4lbs (1.8kg) heavier than the German MG08. Its two main types of tripod mounts weighed about the same as the gun, some 23lbs (10.4kg) lighter than the MG08's sled; and its rate of fire and maximum effective range were still roughly comparable to those of contemporary water-cooled German and British guns.

Throughout the four-year Calvary on the Western Front the Hotchkiss earned an equivalent place in the affections of the French *poilu* to those other classic designs in their own armies. One of the most oft-quoted examples of its endurance occurred in spring 1916 at Verdun, where a two-gun section, isolated by the tide of battle, held off waves of German infantry for ten days and nights. Each is reported to have fired over 75,000 rounds; and both were in excellent order when relief finally arrived. The memoirs of the already-quoted Sgt.Maj.Lafond, a prewar Territorial Hussar NCO who later served with the machine gun units of the Colonial Infantry, include a number of interesting descriptions of the Hotchkiss in action:

"It is the signal. The wave jumps from the trenches and dashes forward. We must fire. Our three guns have already begun their rattle and are spraying the terrain before the enemy's trenches close to the ground, probing the loopholes, mowing the parapets and cutting the last of the barbed wire. 'Lengthen the range. . . On the second position. . . Further. . .On the third; on the fortified emplacement; to the left of the woods. . .Fire, fire, fire, nom de Dieu!' The wonderful little machine devours without a skip the endless munitions which the crew have difficulty in bringing to it."

By 1916 the organisation of dedicated machine gun companies within the French infantry had been stabilised. Georges Lafond again: *"Machine gunners are an element apart, a sort of elite. They feel somewhat superior to - or at least different from - the ordinary companies. Then, too, there is their insignia. The insignia is the bauble, the jewel, of the soldier. It is a real satisfaction to have something on the uniform which distinguishes one from his neighbour. And none of the insignia arouses greater envy than the two small crossed barrels of the machine guns. . . . It takes 150 men, two officers, ten NCOs and 60 horses to serve, supply and transport the eight small guns."*

French Chasseurs à Pied instruct British and Americans in use of the Mle 1914 on the Omnibus tripod. The US soldier standing in left background wears the distinctive leather shoulder pad for carrying the gun, and the insulated barrel changing mitt on his right hand. (NARA)

The gun commander lays the piece for overhead fire by elevating it to a predetermined position which allows fire to pass safely over the heads of friendly troops in the first line trench and fall on the enemy. He will fire a burst or two to confirm the range and test gun functioning. In this case the distinctive flash hider/ blast deflector is fitted to the muzzle; nicknamed the "cow catcher" in the AEF from its resemblance to that feature of old-time American steam locomotives, it is rarely seen in contemporary photographs.

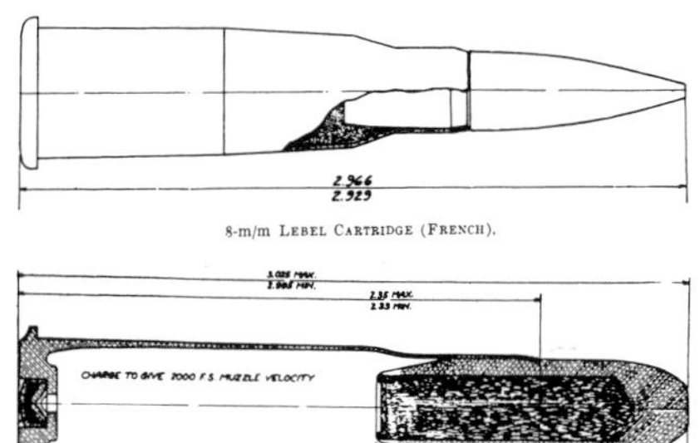

Although the 8mm Type D ball round was widely used against aerial targets, a larger bullet was needed for optimum performance with incendiary, tracer, and explosive fillings. The 8mm case (top) was enlarged at the neck to accommodate an 11mm bullet (bottom); this was used in a specially modified Hotchkiss, and also in modified Vickers guns mounted in aircraft. The success of this so-called "balloon gun" cartridge partly inspired German and American development work on large calibre machine guns. (Springfield Armory National Historic Site)

The basic Hotchkiss crew was five men, with additional ammunition carriers as necessary. The *chef de pièce* commanded the crew and laid the gun; the *tireur* fired it; the *chargeur* loaded it, with the assistance of his *aide-chargeur*; and the *pourvoyeur* relayed ammunition supplies to the loaders. Two gun crews made up a section, and four sections a company - a total of eight guns. From spring 1916 each French infantry battalion had one MG and three rifle companies.

"Lafayette, We Are Here!"

Depending on when they arrived and what sector of the hundreds of miles of trench lines they were destined to occupy, the soldiers and Marines of the American Expeditionary Force were issued with and trained on either British or French machine guns. Although there is understandable prejudice in favour of what one has personally found to be satisfactory in combat, it is fair to say that Doughboys who used the Hotchkiss were just as well pleased with its strengths, and disgusted by its burdens, as those who manned the Vickers. The following account, from the official history of the US 77th Division, is typical of those in any number of unit histories and battle citations:

"The first ray of daylight on October 15th saw Lieutenant Robert Andre, with sixty-seven pounds (sic) of Hotchkiss tripod hanging over his shoulder and thirty-two pounds of boxed ammunition in his hands, crawling and worming his way along the roadside ditch toward the outskirts of St.Juvin. Crawling in his wake was one Rodriguez, of Spanish Main ancestry, snaking along the gun and more ammunition. The two were looking for a spot where 'enfilade fire' could be

ABOVE *Detail of the underside of the barrel showing the interrupted threads on the attachment point at the chamber end, and cut-outs in the five massive steel cooling rings to allow passage of the gas piston.*

RIGHT *The sturdy front sight is rather too wide for maximum accuracy, but is also almost impervious to damage. Note how it is mounted in a dovetail slot; a unit armourer can tap it left or right for a precise "zero".*

ABOVE *The nicely contoured grip and trigger housing, cast from brass and machined to fit the steel receiver; the trigger guard is large enough to accomodate a gloved finger.*

LEFT AND BELOW *After firing a couple of hundred rounds gun function became sluggish; it was necessary to dismantle the gas system, scrub it clean with its special brush, and adjust the chamber setting - screwing in the regulator restricts the chamber volume, causing faster cycling. Note calibrations on the body of the regulator piston; 4.0 is the normal setting, or at least a good starting point.*

The ramp-type rear sight is adjustable for elevation from 250m to 2,000m; there is no adjustment for windage. Its square-cut U-notch is easy to line up with the front sight. Interestingly, the other (right) side of this ramp is marked "Hausse pour cartouche Mle 1886 C", indicating that it is calibrated for the older rifle round; the gunner would use a conversion table to fit the ballistics of the improved Balle D bullet.

delivered. They found it in the rock-strewn front yard of a ruined house, across the interior of which, and through a rear window, ran a perfect line of sight along the entire crest of Hill 182 to the northeast. The ruins gave splendid concealment to the position.

"The Germans, hit from an unexpected quarter, were taken completely by surprise. Rodriguez gave them point-blank all the enfilade fire that a Hotchkiss at full speed can pour from its barrel. They dropped in rows - victims of a very beautiful example of Yankee-made 'surprise effect.' Baffled in their efforts to locate the gun, the succeeding lines of attack fell before it; the Germans were demoralized and our infantry shot down or captured the survivors. This was the end of the counter-attack on St.Juvin."

Hotchkiss Mle 1914 Technical Specifications

Nomenclature	Mitrailleuse Hotchkiss Modele 1914
Manufacturer	Societé de la Fabrication des Armes à Feu Portatives Hotchkiss & Cie.
Calibre	8mm Lebel Mle 1886D(am)
Ammunition	Ball; tracer
System of operation	Gas, open bolt
Cooling	Air
Selector	None; full automatic only
Feed	24- & 30-round metallic strips; 250-round semi-articulated metal belt
Length	51.5ins (1307mm)
Weight, gun	53lbs 11oz (24.35kg) unloaded
Weight, mount	54lbs (24.49kg) Mle 1916 Hotchkiss tripod
Barrel	30.5ins (774mm); 4 grooves, left twist
Sights	Post front; U-notch rear on leaf
Rate of fire	400-600rpm cyclic
Muzzle velocity	2,375fps (723mps)
Max.effective range	1,800m direct, 4,000m indirect

ABOVE *Prepare the gun for loading by pulling back on the generously sized charging handle until the bolt locks at the rear of the receiver; then return the handle to its forward position. In the floor of the brass feed block (left) note the protruding steel sprockets, which engage holes in the feed strips to precisely position each round for chambering.*

LEFT *Using his right thumb to de-clutch the feed sprocket, the assistant pushes a loaded ammunition strip into the feed block on the left side of the receiver. A distinct "click" will be heard and felt when the first cartridge is indexed in the feedway.*

Mechanism

A tour from muzzle to grips may begin in this case - see photos p.93 - with the rarely seen flash hider which we were able to examine during our firing trial. This *cache-flammes* screws onto the muzzle and is held in place by an attached clamping bar. A wedge-shaped expansion chamber inside the main body allows much of the propellant gas to burn off before exiting, and the blast deflector under the front end helps to keep down the firing signature. Because the Hotchkiss is gas operated with a fixed barrel it would not benefit from any sort of muzzle booster. Removal of the flash hider does not alter the functioning of the gun's mechanism in any way.

The barrel group

Because of the necessity for air cooling the *canon-radiateur* (radiator barrel) is quite heavy at 10.6kg (23.3lbs). The five distinctive bronze or steel doughnut-shaped rings over the chamber area pull heat from the chamber and barrel on firing and efficiently dissipate it into the surrounding air. Remarkably, the gun still has a sustainable fire rate of some 200 rounds per minute.

The **front sight**, mounted on a thick steel band around the barrel, sits on a moderately tall post so as to align with the rear sight atop the receiver. The prominent **gas cylinder support block** is machined from steel and "sweated" onto the barrel over the place where a gas exit hole has been drilled. This acts as a channel for propellant gas to enter the cylinder and act on the piston. The cylinder and its

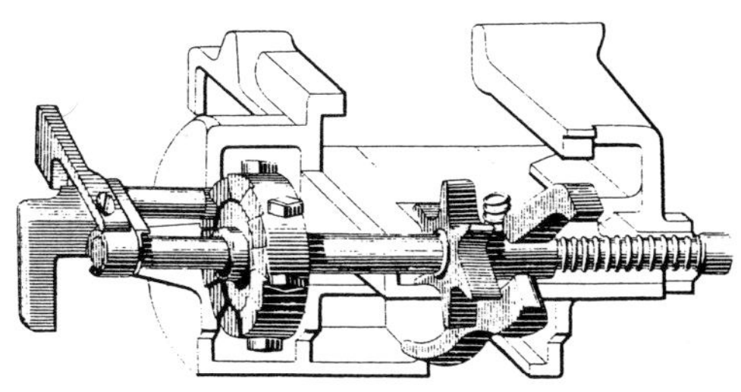

Diagram showing the gearing inside the feed block; the comparison to a maritime geared windlass is particularly appropriate. (Courtesy Gerard Demaison)

A full 24-round strip in position ready for firing. Made from brass or steel, these relatively flimsy strips were superior to fabric belts as they were unaffected by cold or moisture - though not impervious to either mud or corrosive gas. Under the barrel radiator rings, note the gas piston.

screw-adjusted regulator piston form an expansion chamber where the piston end of the bolt carrier is violently kicked backward with each shot. A numerical scale is engraved on the gas cylinder to facilitate resetting after removal for cleaning.

The interrupted threads for attachment of the barrel to the receiver are fairly comparable to modern quick-change designs; stop pins ensure that the barrel is correctly positioned. A hefty combination wrench is kept with the gun for removing and replacing the barrel and gas system. A spare barrel accompanied each gun into action, and additional barrels were kept with the gun limber. It was changed as necessary for efficient operation during sustained fire missions, particularly in critical overhead fire to support friendly troops.

The receiver group

The *boite de culasse* or receiver is a beautiful piece of intricate machine work, quite different from the slab-sided boxes of the Maxim and Vickers. The inside is divided into three horizontal guide compartments, with the breech block (bolt) supported by the upper guides as it cycles; the middle guide contains the piston, and the lower guide the recoil spring. The left side has guides for the cocking handle and a recess for the ejector. Near the front of the receiver is a transverse opening to accept the feed block. The empty case deflector is pinned to the right side of the receiver, also acting as a shield over the ejection port.

Positioned above the elevating gear attachment point, and not to be confused with the tripod cradle mounting trunnions, **recoil blocks** are driven into the sides of the receiver and held in place with taper pins. These are the key to avoiding excessive headspace, which causes ruptured cartridges; they had to be kept well oiled in operation, and replaced when worn. The **rear sight**, of the ramp style common to many infantry rifles, is mounted at the top and front of the receiver above the tripod mounting trunnions.

The **piston and bolt-carrier** is another fine piece of machined steel. Its lugs and cams actuate the feeding, firing, extracting and ejecting operations as it is blown back by gas on firing and driven forward by the recoil spring. It carries the *culasse mobile* - breech block or **bolt** - linked by a swinging lock arm. Part of the genius of Benet's design is the absolute safety against cartridge detonation until the bolt is securely locked behind the chambered cartridge; only then is the piston free to move fully forward, causing the firing pin to be driven into the primer. Similarly, on detonation the bolt does not unlock until the piston has moved a short distance rearward, allowing time for gas pressure to drop; this brief delay minimises failure to extract, torn rims and separated cases.

View through the right side showing the first cartridge indexed in the feedway. The flared rectangular brass well at the left is the deflector on the ejection port; the button-shaped steel piece inside prevents excessive wear to the soft brass.

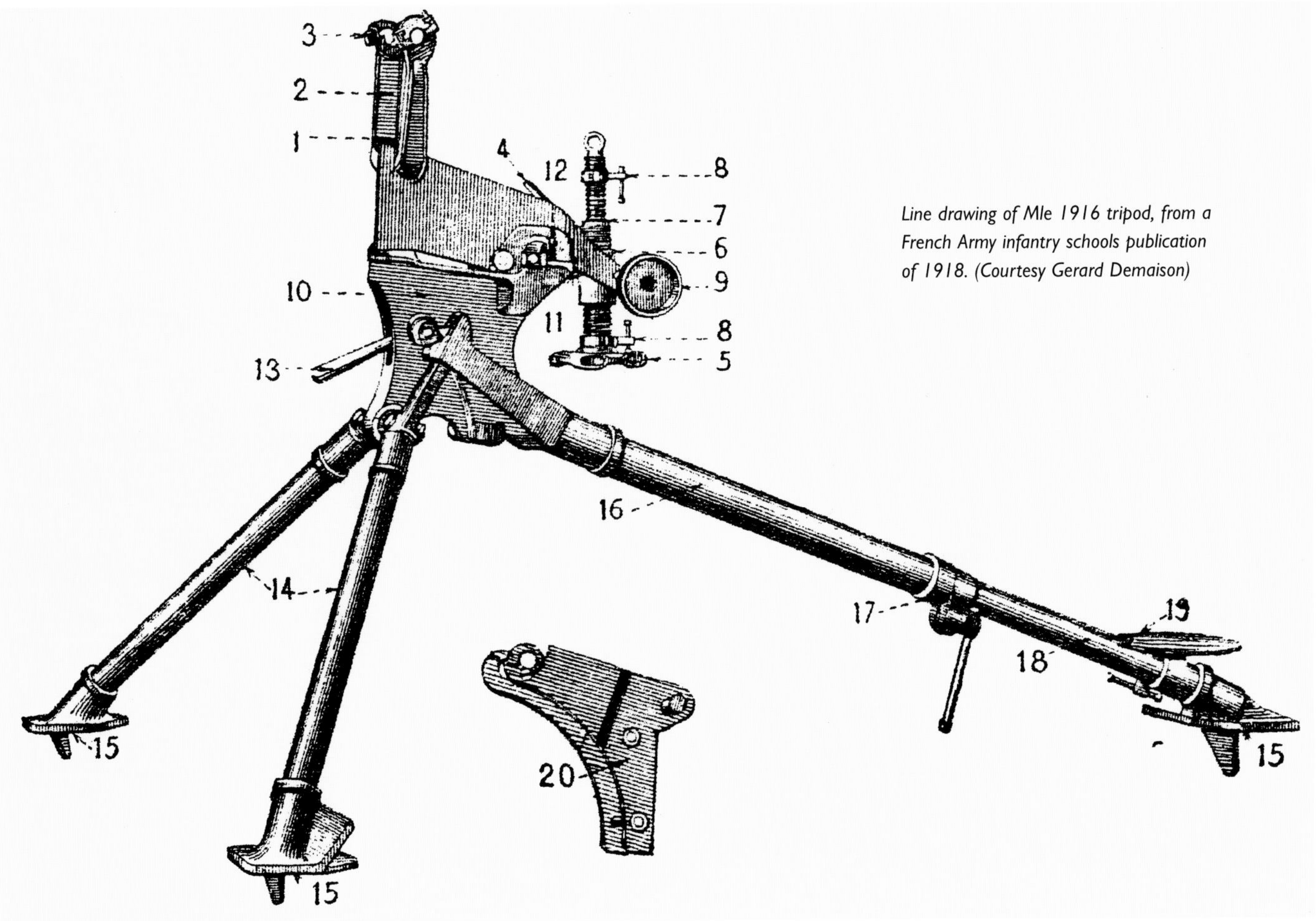

Line drawing of Mle 1916 tripod, from a French Army infantry schools publication of 1918. (Courtesy Gerard Demaison)

The **recoil spring**, at the bottom of the receiver, is a long, heavy spiral. Compressed upon firing, it pushes against a projection on the underside of the piston/bolt carrier to drive it forward for feeding and locking. A rectangular guide inside the spring and running part way along its length keeps it from kinking under compression.

The **pistol grip and trigger housing** group slides neatly into the bottom of the receiver. Its main function is to provide a trip mechanism for the piston/bolt carrier. The grip itself, smoothly cast in solid brass, is both a stylish accent to the blue steel receiver and a comfortable handful. Beware, however, of gripping it with bare hands on freezing mornings, or you are likely to leave some skin behind.

Also made from cast brass fitted with steel working parts, the *mechanisme d'alimentation* (**feed block**) is particularly interesting when compared to that of the Maxim: it is fascinating to see how Benet fashioned a very efficient alternative to the patented, and problematical, cloth belts. Starting with a ratcheted windlass, he devised a cog-and-gear device that would move the metal feed strips through the gun in precise movements. Each cycle of the piston acts on the operating wheel, positioning a cartridge held in the strip to be pushed by the bolt up and into the chamber. Twenty-four compartments in the metal strips hold each cartridge firmly and in exactly the right position.

The **feed strips** are largely unaffected by moisture, hardy enough for repeated use, yet cheap enough to throw away when damaged. They can be attached one to another during the operation of the gun, giving almost continuous firing. The loading tool provided in the gunner's kit is a large rectangular metal plate with fittings to hold the strips while cartridges are positioned by hand as far as possible into the locking clips. Moving the two handles inward forces the cartridges the rest of the way into position. This tool can also be used without modification to load the articulated 250-round feed bands.

The mounting

The standard French *affut-trepied* mounts of the Great War were the Mle 1915 Omnibus, characterised by a prominent elevating handwheel in the vertical plane; and the somewhat lighter and simpler Mle 1916 Hotchkiss. Both provided excellent elevation control and adequate traverse, and both would also accomodate the notoriously complicated Mle 1907T St.Etienne heavy machine gun. The Mle 1916, seen in the accompanying line drawing from a French manual, differs from the US-made Standard Parts Co. model of 1916 shown in our colour photographs principally in having a limited traversing scale.

Detail of the traversing and elevating mechanism of the improved Mle 1916 tripod. Note the scale on the traversing plate, helping the gunner to pre-register targets for later engagement. (NARA)

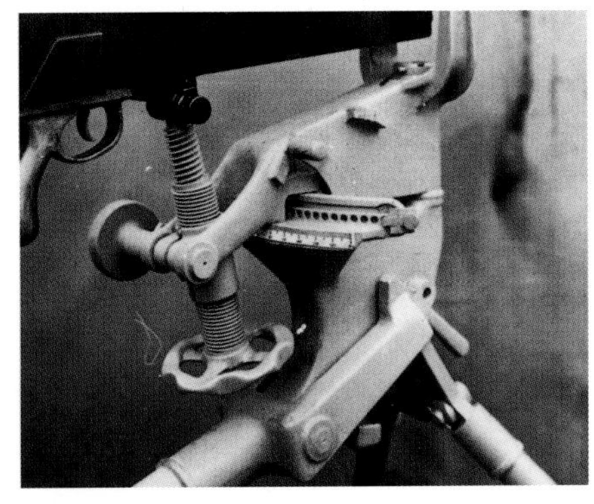

ABOVE LEFT *Detail of the 360-degree traverse ring of the US-made M1916 tripod. Locked into one of the holes, nearside centre, is a traversing stop; these could be set to provide a positive safety factor when the gun was laid for enfilade fire along the front of the Allied wire.*

ABOVE RIGHT *The jamming handle, seen here in its locked position, could be thrown forward to allow unrestricted traverse in emergencies.*

OPPOSITE TOP *Detail of the locking system, removed from the gun. The bolt (top) is shown in its fully locked position with the rear locking flap down.*

OPPOSITE BOTTOM *Firing the Hotchkiss. With a non-reciprocating cocking handle, and modern smokeless powder (invented by Frenchman Paul Vielle and perfected in 1884), the only visible indications of firing are dust kicked up by muzzle blast, and an empty case ejecting to the right.*

Although the Mle 1916 was a formidably heavy 24.49kg (54lbs), it was exceptionally stable for long range shooting. Its front legs, although not individually adjustable, could be swung up or down for a higher or lower profile as needed. The rear leg also moves up and down and telescopes; and supports a thoughtful though inadequately small "bicycle seat", putting the gunner's weight to good use for additional stability.

As with the Maxim and Vickers, various trench and AA mounts of growing sophistication were developed by 1918; these included a single-spike picquet monopod, and the *bipied-support* bipod used together with a detachable shoulder stock. The *affut-trepied Jean Fourche 105* was eventually made available for anti-aircraft use.

Cycle of operation

Quite unlike the closed-bolt, recoil-operated Maxim and Vickers, the Hotchkiss is a much simpler "slam-fire" gun firing from an open bolt. It fires by driving a cartridge in a straight line out of the feed strip and into the chamber as the bolt runs forward under pressure of the recoil spring. The feed wheel advances one half of the feeding movement with a ratchet preventing rebound.

When the bolt has travelled fully forward the bolt lock is in position above the recoil blocks; the locking cam of the piston causes the rear end of the bolt lock to tilt down in front of the recoil blocks. The piston continues forward, causing the firing pin to be driven into the cartridge primer - this cannot occur until the bolt is fully locked.

After the cartridge detonates and the bullet passes the gas port in the barrel, gas enters the expansion chamber and begins to drive the piston rearward, beginning compression of the recoil spring. Action of the piston also pulls the firing pin back inside the bolt head as the lock swings up and clear of the recoil blocks. The entire bolt and piston assembly is then free to run fully rearward in the receiver.

As this is occurring, the expended case is withdrawn from the receiver and ejected through the right side port. The feed wheel advances the second half of its cycle, positioning the next cartridge for chambering. The travel of the piston is stopped when it strikes the breech cover. Then, unless the trigger is released to engage the sear, the firing cycle begins once again - between 400 and 600 times per minute, or seven to ten shots per second, depending on the setting of the gas regulator and the condition of the gun.

The feed strip runs through from left to right and drops out of the gun; its departure allows an arrestor to spring up and stop the piston with the bolt open, allowing loading of a fresh strip, protecting against "cook-off" of a chambered cartridge, and allowing some air circulation through the barrel.

Rotating the elevation handwheel turns a spiral screw for exceptionally fine ranging. The adjustable clamp just above is another safety device, ensuring that the gun is not depressed too far when firing over friendly troops.

Preparing to fire

Place the tripod and ensure that the legs are level and firmly grounded; some digging is almost always necessary. Attach the gun to the tripod, and test movement of the traversing and elevating mechanism. Apply oil to the gun and tripod as necessary: according to the American manual, "The receiver should always be flooded with oil while firing and cleaned and reoiled after firing."

Obviously, as with all weapons which have been taken into rough terrain, check the bore to ensure it is free of obstructions - mud jammed in the muzzle may cause the barrel to explode on firing. If the flash hider is being used, make sure it

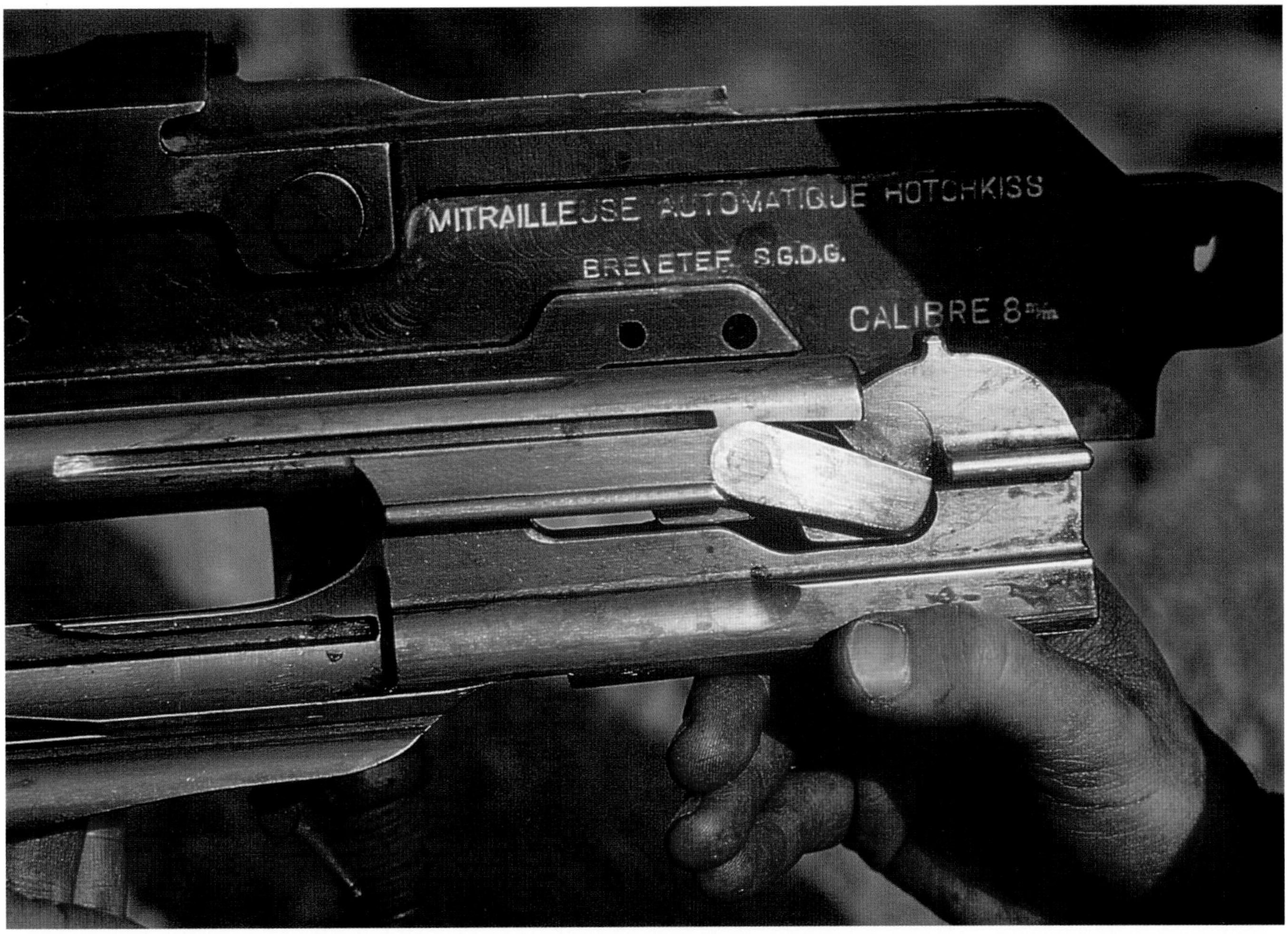
MITRAILLEUSE AUTOMATIQUE HOTCHKISS
BREVETEE S.G.D.G.
CALIBRE 8 m/m

Note the puff of smoke from the gas system under the barrel. Hammering away at a brisk cyclic rate of some 550rpm, the heavy gun/tripod system vibrates only slighty from recoil. Muzzle blast is hardly perceptible to the gunner, but noticeably harsher on the ears of the loader crouched further out to the side.

is screwed on all the way and clamped. Make sure the barrel lock is in the down (locked) position; and check the gas regulator setting - 4.0 is the usual starting point. Have the spare barrel, gunner's tools and oil can ready to hand. Check the feed strips to ensure that all cartridges are properly positioned and free of dirt.

The gun must be in the cocked position for loading; if necessary, pull back the cocking handle until the bolt and piston lock fully rearward, then return the handle to the forward position. The loader inserts the feed strip, with the cartridges uppermost, into the left side of the gun, carefully aligning it with the guides in the feed block. He pushes it in until it locks into place, automatically positioning the first round for feeding. *Caution* - there is no mechanical safety, and the gun is now ready to shoot.

It may be necessary, with a new barrel or with one that has not been recently tested with the gun, to adjust the **gas regulator**. Start by removing the regulator assembly entirely and firing a couple of shots to blast the gas orifice clear. Replace the assembly, set it at 4.0, and fire a single shot. If the gun's functioning shows symptoms of insufficient energy such as failure to eject or uncontrolled automatic fire, screw the regulator down several turns and try again. Repeat until the action is satisfactory, then screw the regulator in two more turns; record this setting for future use. Good judgement must be used to avoid the harmful effects of too much gas - symptoms are excessive speed causing pounding of the recoiling parts, and cartridge rims marked, cut or even torn through by the extractor.

If **unloading** a partially consumed feed strip, pull the cocking handle back as far as it will go and hold it there. This will declutch the feed mechanism and allow the feed strip to be withdrawn through the left side. Inspect the chamber area to ensure no round is present. Then, with the gun pointed in a safe direction, hold the cocking handle while pulling the trigger and allow the bolt to ride home.

Firing the Hotchkiss

With the gun loaded and the sights correctly positioned for direct fire, the gunner steadies the rear D-handle with his left hand, holds the pistol grip with his right, and squeezes the trigger.

One of the most remarkable aspects of the Hotchkiss is its sedate, almost monotonously regular rate of fire. It chatters away loudly and purposefully, but with little external indication of its functioning. Unlike the Maxim and Vickers, its cocking handle does not reciprocate during firing, so its table of malfunctions is based on observing the position of the bolt through the ejection port. This indicates the three main types of stoppage and cues the gunner to initiate the appropriate immediate action.

As can be seen in the accompanying photographs, a fair amount of dust is raised at the muzzle by the blast and bullet shock wave. (This would be minimised by use of the flash hider, but owner Charles Erb wasn't anxious to have this very rare and nearly mint-condition accessory put to the test.) Muzzle report is easy on the gunner, but the other crewmen crouching by his side get quite a pounding on the eardrums. Short, engine-like puffs of smoke shoot out of the gas system with each round fired, and the feed strip methodically stutters across the receiver. Empties are energetically flipped out the right side of the gun.

The recoil effect of the 8mm rifle cartridges on this 110lb (49.8kg) gun and tripod assembly is, of course, very slight. However, due to recoil-induced settling of the mount attention must be paid soon after firing the first couple of feed strips. Stop and carefully check the sights, adjusting elevation and traverse to ensure that the gun is still exactly on target. This should be repeated periodically, and with increasing frequency when firing over the heads of friendly troops.

AA machine gun team from the US 1st Balloon Co. at St.Veul, France. After years of improvised AA mounts the sturdy Affut-trepied Jean Fourche 105 appeared, allowing quick all-round aiming. (Author's collection)

According to contemporary documentation, the gun can be fired almost indefinitely at a rate of some 200rpm. In the words of the US Ordnance Department's January 1918 handbook for the Model 1914: "The barrel will attain a temperature of about 400 degrees Celsius, which is a dark red. At this point it dissipates heat just as fast as it is generated. This only occurs after long continuous fire. During continuous fire the barrel should be changed after every 700 to 1,000 rounds, except in critical situations. If water is sponged on the barrel, the fire may be continued longer without injury to the barrel."

Despite being air-cooled the Hotchkiss can be fired almost indefinitely at a rate of 200 rounds per minute, making it almost as valuable for indirect barrage work as water-cooled guns. Here the loader is joining up 24-round strips as the gun fires; and note the sharply tapered shape of the broad-based 8mm Lebel cartridge, here with the streamlined D-type bullet adopted in 1912.

Our *poilus* of the reconstructed 151eme RI initially used cardboard targets set up at a range of about 200m to try both "searching fire", by manipulating the elevating handwheel on the tripod, and "traversing fire", by releasing the traverse lock and tapping the gun left and right while shooting. The fine elevating mechanism enabled precise placement of shots, but traverse would benefit from having a similar control.

We then decided to do a more visually interesting test using cinderblock pieces set up some 50m from the gun. While this may not sound all that challenging, it is roughly equivalent to hitting a helmeted head at about half the length of a football field using sights that are way off calibration. It took several bursts - and much wasted film - to dial the tripod-mounted gun right into the target, but the results speak for themselves in the accompanying photos. It would do no good to hide behind anything short of a stone wall or a couple of feet of hard-packed dirt.

Changing barrels

A pair of thick leather or asbestos mitts with chain mail palms was issued for protection against burns when removing a hot barrel, as well as a healthy-sized combination wrench for the barrel and gas system.

Unload the gun and recock if necessary. Turn the barrel lock all the way to the rear (unlocked) position. Place the dismounting wrench over the gas cylinder support, with the handle extending to the left of the receiver. Push down firmly and turn it slightly until the barrel stop pin strikes the receiver. Because of its interrupted threads the barrel may now be pulled out of its receiver socket.

Place the new barrel in the receiver and turn it to the right until the stop pin strikes the top of the receiver. Be sure to turn the barrel lock down into its locked position.

Headspace is not readily adjustable. Barrels and bolts for each gun were assembled and gauged by an armourer before going into action; he also changed the recoil blocks when headspace became excessive due to wear - this was another reason to "keep the receiver flooded with oil."

The destructive power of the 198-grain 8mm Balle D ammunition travelling at some 2,300 feet per second is illustrated here by disintegration of a stack of cinder blocks; one short burst at a range of about 50 meters immediately reduced them to dust.

US artillerymen in France with a very common improvised AA mount consisting of a wagon wheel attached to a buried post; the Hotchkiss itself is mounted on the cradle of an Omnibus ground tripod. The spare parts and tool roll hangs from the elevating handwheel. (USACMH)

Simpler internally than its Maxim-type contemporaries, the Hotchkiss requires a smaller gunner's tool kit. Note the cleaning brushes, oil can, and small spares; and the robust wrench, with one large U-shaped end for dismounting the barrel and a smaller hexagonal end for the gas system.

Conclusion

A heavy and rock-steady combination of gun and tripod, the world's first efficient air-cooled heavy machine gun is admirably reliable and accurate. It is easy to appreciate the affection that Sgt.Maj.Georges Lafond and his comrades of "Compagnie Casanova" felt for this defender of Verdun - a cleanly designed, beautifully constructed weapon which steadfastly fired on and on, without demanding their precious water for coolant.

Credits

Gun owner, Charles Erb, Fredericktown, PA; gunner, Mark Meader, Hyattsville, MD; assistant gunner, Paul Smith, Mt. Airy, MD; ammunition carrier, Brian Pohanka, Alexandria, VA; location assistant, John Exley IV, Mechanicsville, VA; uniforms & equipment, personal collections of the gun crew, members of the re-enactment group 151eme Régiment d'Infanterie; range, Great War Association, Shimpstown, PA. Primary research source: Lafond, Georges, *Covered with Mud and Glory*.

STRIPPING THE HOTCHKISS

The gun can be field stripped without any special tools.

First, clear it by pulling the cocking handle all the way back, which disengages the feed strip gear. Pull the strip out, and check that the chamber is empty. Hold on to the cocking handle, pull the trigger, and allow the bolt to ride home.

Begin the field strip by turning the retaining pin until it aligns with its cut-out key; push in the recoil spring extension inside the bottom of the rear handle; and withdraw the pin.

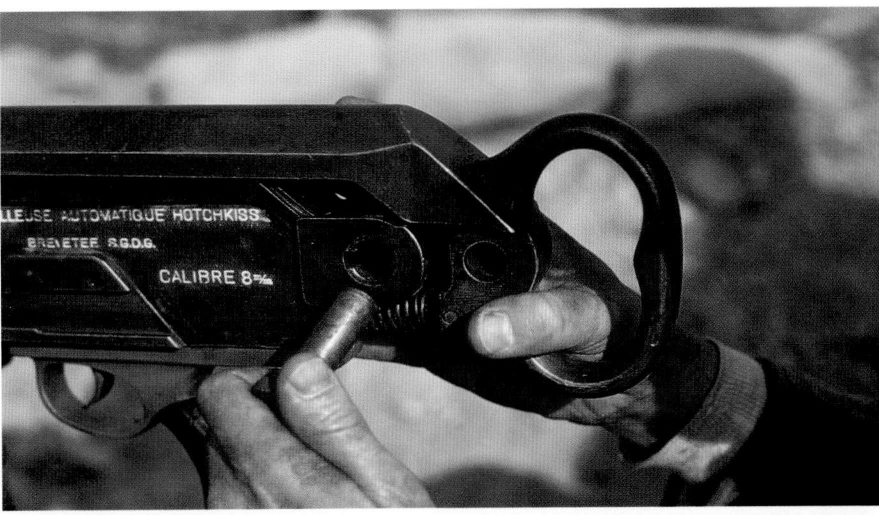

Pull the rear handle back; this will slide off the top cover and also withdraw the recoil spring.

Remove the pistol grip and trigger housing by pulling it slightly backward until it clears the rear of the receiver, then tipping it downward. Tip the trigger group forward and remove it from the housing.

Pull the cocking handle slightly back; then remove the feed block retaining clip by sliding it to the rear.

Grasp the feed block firmly and pull it out from the left side of the receiver.

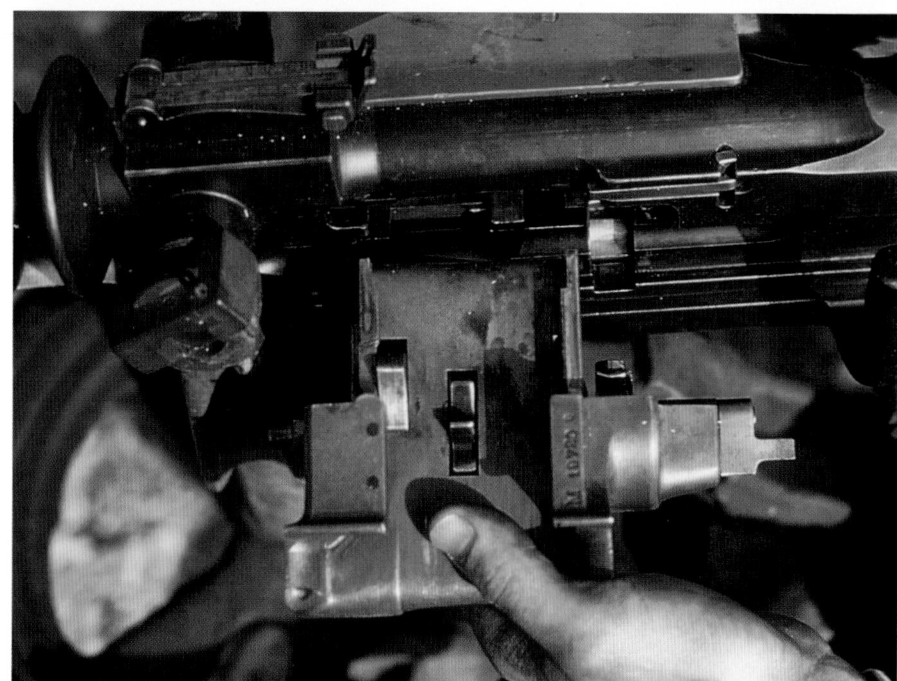

Use the cocking handle to slide the bolt and operating rod carrier to the rear until it can be withdrawn from the receiver. This photo shows the relationship between the receiver and the gas piston slide, bolt and bolt carrier.

Detail showing (bottom to top) the bolt carrier, bolt and firing pin. Camming surfaces cut in the side of the gas piston/bolt carrier operate the feed block with each round fired, turning the sprocket wheel to move the feed strip.

Field strip layout (top to bottom, left to right):
Receiver and barrel group, bolt and firing pin, gas piston/bolt carrier, receiver cover and attached recoil spring, feed block, pistol grip and trigger group, retaining clip, cocking handle and feed strip. No further disassembly is needed for routine care and cleaning.

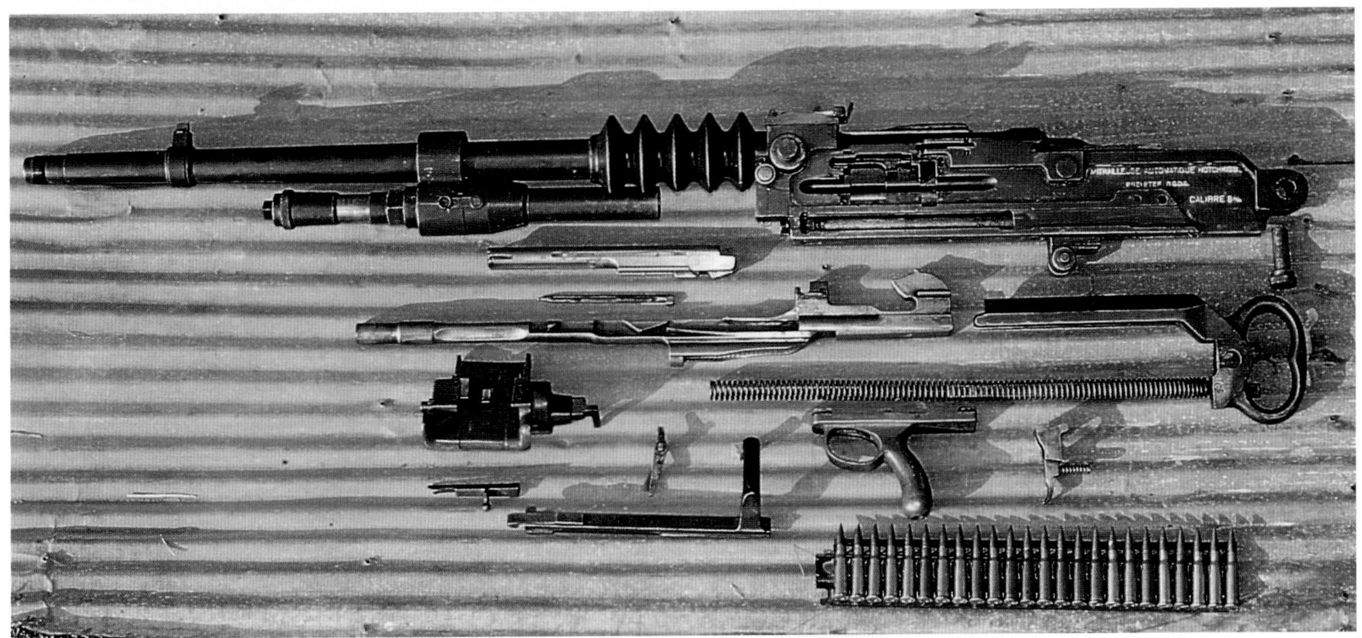

Although by no means a quick-change system, exchanging a worn or overheated barrel is fast and easy compared with water-cooled designs. Here the combination wrench is being used to twist the barrel and attached gas cylinder a quarter-turn on its interrupted threads for removal. Due to exceptionally low barrel erosion from the copper-zinc alloy French bullet, barrel life is listed as a remarkable 15,000 rounds.

CHAUCHAT Mle 1915

"The automatic rifle squads were making their Chauchats rattle like machine guns. Near me was the fifth squad, commanded by Corporal Chas. H.Luckenbaugh. Gunner Parsons, when he could no longer see an enemy from the trench, climbed up on the parapet and fired his heavy Chauchat from his shoulder. There was no yelling, swearing, or cries of pain, but each man attended quietly, with spirit and determination, to defeating the enemy. They were fighting without passion or hatred, and apparently with complete forgetfulness of their own safety. Both sides had them, but no bombs were thrown. On our side it was strictly rifle and Chauchat fire, and rifles and machine guns were used by the Germans."
(1st Lt.C.W.Ryan, 30th & 38th Infantry, US 3rd Inf.Div., quoted Edmund L.Butts, *The Keypoint of the Marne*, 1930)

September 1916: a khaki-uniformed Chauchat gunner of the French Army's 53rd Colonial Infantry Regiment. In addition to his machine rifle - of early pattern, without flash hider - he is holding his issue Ruby semi-automatic pistol. The distinctive crescent-shaped leather pouches each carried two magazines; they were inadequate to protect the flimsy magazines from crushing when gunners dropped prone, with consequent feed problems. (NARA)

The French Chauchat machine rifle is the object of some of the most outspoken criticism ever heaped upon an automatic weapon. Phrases such as "undoubtedly quite the worst", "the clumsiest and balkiest ever encountered", "most defective" and "abysmal" crop up with alarming regularity in technical books and postwar history journals. On the other hand, there are many officially documented instances of Chauchat gunners dispatching Germans in droves to turn the tide of battle; and a new book - *Honour Bound*, by Gerard Demaison & Yves Buffetaut - shows that such vitriolic criticisms may somewhat overstate the reality.

Development

The Hotchkiss models of 1900 and 1914 had proven reliable and effective heavy machine guns; but the French military were looking for a lighter, cheaper weapon to be mass-produced and placed in the hands of large numbers of infantrymen. Period military publications contained a number of articles by French tacticians promoting the concept of "walking fire" - advancing soldiers firing bursts from the hip at enemy trenches in an attempt to keep the defenders' heads down.

One approach to a more portable weapon was the Benet-Mercié Mle 1909 machine rifle or "light Hotchkiss"; another was the Berthier 1908. While both were reportedly accurate and acceptably reliable when properly cared for, they were expensive to make and complicated to use. Another avenue for exploration was the rapidly emerging industrial technique of hydraulic stamping to cut and form heavy sheet metal; small arms produced in this manner, rather than by the traditional milling and boring from solid billets of steel, would lend themselves to cheap mass production.

Between 1903 and 1910 French Army Capt.Louis Chauchat and master armourer Charles Sutter developed several semi- and full-automatic rifles at the Atelier de Construction de Puteaux. These culminated in a strikingly simple weapon made from tubing and riveted sheet metal, which showed sufficient promise in testing to warrant further work. By 1913 this Chauchat-Sutter Fusil Mitrailleur (machine rifle) was performing well enough to be put into production by the MAS factory at St.Etienne. The first 100, initially intended as ground weapons, were in fact pressed into service for use by aircraft observers as the aerial arms race quickly escalated.

Fusil Mitrailleur Mle 1915 CSRG with bipod extended. Made from steel tubing and stampings with a minimum of machine work, the gun's main virtues were low cost and speed of manufacture.

"The Rock of the Marne" - an 8mm CSRG takes centre stage in this official US Army historical poster depicting men of the 3rd Infantry Division at Mézy in July 1918. (USACMH

Reconstruction - Meuse-Argonne offensive, September-October 1918: An AEF "Doughboy" armed with a Mle 1915 CSRG, operating as a hunter-killer of German light machine gun teams. The long, heavy gun with its big bottom-mounted magazine is awkward to carry in action without the support of the sling.

The odd placing of the "tool handle" foregrip immediately in front of the pistol grip is comfortable only for prone fire with both elbows supported.

ABOVE LEFT AND RIGHT *The left side of the receiver shows how mass production techniques of hydraulic stamping, welding and riveting were used in the gun's manufacture. The sling swivels are well placed, and the relatively uninterrupted left surface allowed the CSRG to be carried comfortably over the shoulder when out of the line. The star marking and "SIDARME" identify no.18774 as one of the 20,000-odd guns manufactured by FAMH at St.Chamond when Gladiator could no longer keep up with demand. Note the large magazine release bar, notched to support the ends of the fully folded bipod.*

Into mass production

By the end of 1914 the prewar French disdain for any tactic but the assault had decimated their army, eventually forcing a sober re-examination of the bitter realities of this new kind of war. Between the parallel trench systems of the static front lines artillery and machine guns dominated the ruined landscape of No Man's Land. Firepower was the key ingredient in the limited advances achieved, and bolt-action rifles were badly outclassed. The call went out for machine guns - as many as could be obtained, as quickly as possible. Louis Chauchat, now a colonel, had the logical solution.

An emergency order for 50,000 Chauchat-Sutter machine rifles was signed by Gen.Joffre, Chief of the General Staff, in 1915. The contract was awarded to Gladiator, a Parisian bicycle and motorcar company, for a ground version with wooden stock and bipod. The production model was a modification of the Mle 1913 CSFM, most notably in having its distinctive crescent-shaped magazine (determined by the abrupt taper of the 8mm Lebel cartridge) relocated underneath the receiver. This new weapon was designated Fusil Mitrailleur 1915 CSRG - after Chauchat, Sutter, production manager Paul Ribeyrolles, and the Gladiator company. Col.Chauchat himself was assigned to supervise the entire process of tooling up and production.

Much scorn has been heaped on the production of the Mle 1915, with tales of parts and assemblies being made by all sorts of inferior subcontractors. However, as described by Demaison & Buffetaut, all but the barrel (Chatellerault) and its sleeve (Peugeot) were in fact made on site by Gladiator; and it seems unlikely that the colonel would have accepted standards lower than necessary to ensure proper function of his namesake weapon. Nevertheless, there were inherent flaws in the flimsy magazines which - inexplicably - were never satisfactorily corrected although clearly identified in the 1913 guns.

Serious start-up problems meant that it was autumn 1916 before acceptable weapons began to be delivered in quantity. Field reports were particularly critical of breakage of bolts and extractors due to inferior materials or defective heat treatment. The completed product was undeniably ugly and awkward, with little attention given to the finish of exposed metal parts or the wooden furniture. With its slab buttstock, square pistol grip, "tool handle" foregrip, receiver tubing and sheet metal stampings, the CSRG was not likely to inspire immediate confidence in the men to whom it was issued.

Cutaway diagram with major parts and assemblies of the CSRG identified in French, from the September 1917 booklet Le Fusil Mitrailleur 1915, CSRG *published by the École des Specialités d'Armée. (Courtesy Gerard Demaison)*

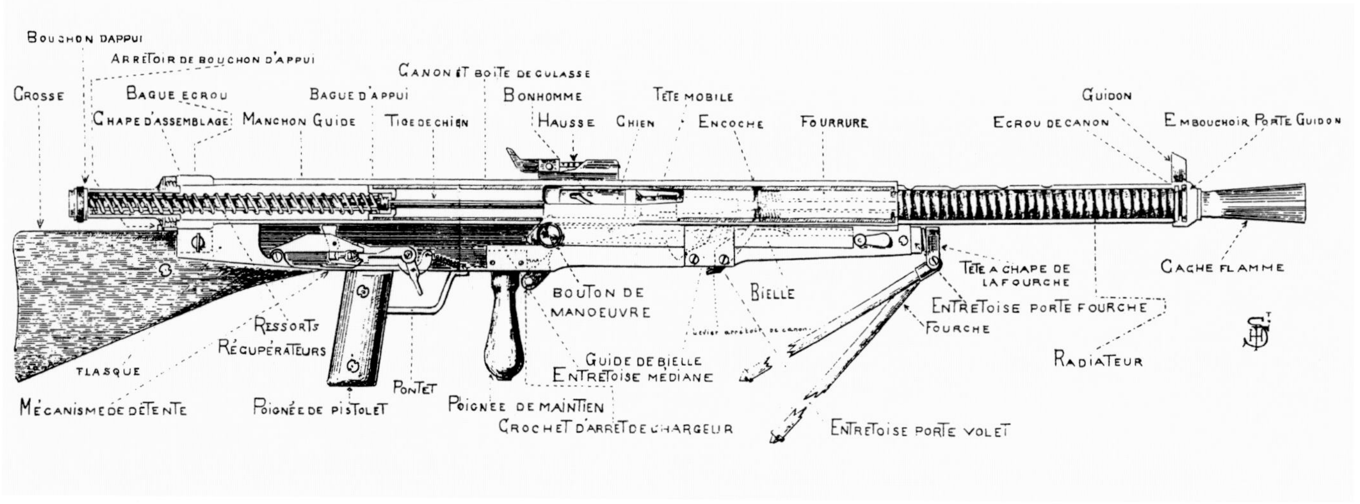

École de Chauchat

An automatic rifle school was set up in a suburb of Paris with the aim of training instructors who would, in turn, train two-man combat teams in field units. The week-long programme of instruction was soon doubled so that the gunner and loader could be better versed in the many eccentricities of the new weapon.

Central to the training was exhaustive drill in the technique of "walking fire" whereby the gunner and his assistant would walk side by side toward the objective, firing and reloading without breaking stride. This was no easy task even on a level training field far from the enemy, due to the extremely long and front-heavy gun and its inconveniently arranged magazine feed; the distractions of being fired at while stumbling through mud, shell holes and barbed wire were apparently discounted by the theorists. The gunner's task was eased somewhat by use of a sling to help position the weapon, but care was still needed to provide sufficient support to the buttstock. Operating as it did on the "long recoil" principal (see below), failure to cycle would result if the gun was allowed to "float" on firing.

Illustration from a book published in 1920, purporting to show individual French infantrymen with their weapons and equipment but actually a cut-and-retouch job from a single photo of a late war machine gun killer team. From the left it shows the CSRG gunner; a VB rifle grenadier; a rifleman/ ammo carrier; a bomber holding two hand grenades; and a second rifleman/ ammo carrier. By 1918 co-ordinated Chauchat, rifle grenade and hand grenade tactics down to squad level were proving effective in eliminating the increasing numbers of German light and heavy machine gun teams by direct assault. (Author's collection)

The second most important firing position was prone, bipod-supported. This was where the truly abysmal ergonomics of the CSRG forced themselves on the gunner's attention. Lying behind it with the stock in the shoulder pocket and his right eye behind the sights, a normal sized Frenchman would find his cheekbone in contact with the receiver housing plug, and firing the gun at this point would immediately result in painful bruising (which was common enough to get its own nickname - *la gifle*, "the smack"). This confidence-shattering characteristic was partially overcome by teaching the gunner to cant his body sharply to the left of the gun while placing his cheek forward of the rear collar and plug. It was also emphasized that the stock must be held tightly against the shoulder to provide the necessary resistance on recoil to allow full cycling of the long-recoil action. All of this was awkward and unnatural, but necessary.

Interestingly, most marksmanship instruction was said to be concentrated on semi-automatic fire as the most efficient and potentially effective; while this was probably true, and saved ammunition, it would seem to contradict the very purpose of developing an automatic rifle. A strong clue may be found in reports from extensive firing tests at the time, which reveal a disturbing inadequacy in rate of fire. Even a perfectly clean and well lubricated gun would usually seize up from overheating after firing little more than 300 rounds in full-automatic. Gunners reported having to wait several minutes for the barrel and sleeve to cool down to the point where the barrel could slide forward again to allow locking. Dirty and carbonised guns would lock up much more quickly, no doubt leaving the gunner cursing foully and protected only by his pipsqueak pistol.

Reports of guns returned to the factory for repair with more than apparent battle damage became more frequent. It is not surprising that enraged gunners should have clubbed their balky Chauchats with anything to hand in an attempt to unjam the action, or in simple frustration, even though the French authorities ordered "severe reprisals" against soldiers caught abusing their CSRGs. (They did not, apparently, initiate similar action against the designer and the factory for delivering systematically inadequate weapons. . .)

The documented inaccuracy of the gun, caused by its long recoil system, inadequate bipod and poorly placed and aligned sights, was compensated for by an emphasis on close-in fighting. Much of the range work was with individual targets at 100 to 200m, with a maximum range of 400m for firing at grouped targets representing German light machine gun teams.

Optimistically large quantities of ammunition accompanied the two crewmen in special carriers. The gunner had a pair of sturdy half-moon shaped leather pouches on his waist

29 August 1918, France: men of the US 137th Infantry Regiment, 35th Division, fire their Mle 1915 CSRG at German positions from a well-protected outpost near Amphersbach. The assistant is ready to feed another magazine into the gun; note the strap of his special musette bag. (NARA)

ABOVE *The French-made M1918 conversion to handle American .30-06 ammunition is identified by its ribbed box magazine and the foregrip moved forward of the magazine; this one is optimistically fitted with the clamp-on AA sights. The consequences of the ill-advised conversion from the tapered Lebel cartridge to the more powerful, almost straight-sided .30-06 round were compounded by production errors leading to most of these 18,000 guns having chambers of incorrect depth and inferior craftsmanship. The abysmal failure of the US-calibre version is one of the main reasons for the Chauchat's bad reputation.*

The Hotchkiss "Portative" in use by Indian cavalry of the British Army on the Somme, 1916; it was issued one per troop, i.e. 12 per regiment. The US Army designated it Model 1909 Benet-Mercié machine rifle. (NARA)

belt and suspenders, each carrying two 20-round magazines. An additional 12 magazines were carried in the first model special knapsack. A later, more common version held eight loaded magazines plus 64 packaged cartridges). The gunner's personal sidearm was a Spanish .32 Ruby semi-auto pistol holstered at the back of the waist belt.

The assistant also wore the special knapsack, and carried an additional four magazines in a well designed musette bag. He was armed with a bolt-action 8mm rifle or carbine which, by necessity of his duties, spent most of its time slung over his back.

"Mud is Enemy No. 1"

The first large scale use of the CSRG occured during the battles on the Somme in summer-autumn 1916. Although it earned some praise, two of the most impassioned criticisms of the gun were its intolerance of the pervasive mud of the battlefield, and the pathetic weakness of its magazines. The many large openings in the magazine and the gun allowed grit and moisture to penetrate every inner recess, combining into an abrasive paste that was fatal to its operation. The use of a protective canvas cover helped alleviate this problem somewhat; but little could - or would - be done about the magazine.

Gunners bitterly denounced the inability of the leather magazine pouches to protect the magazines from compression damage when they fell - as they inevitably must - into the prone position. The feed lips of the magazines were also easily deformed; and the zig-zag follower spring was not strong enough, and quickly lost tension when loaded. It was not until early 1918 that serious efforts were made to find an acceptable alternative magazine, and even then nothing came of it before the war ended.

As if this were not enough, the design of the gun left it prone to a catalogue of malfunctions. Damaged magazines caused failure to feed; dirty ammunition caused failure to chamber, and the bolt could not fully close. Failure to cycle upon firing was caused by overheating, dirt, or carbon fouling binding the barrel group inside its steel bicycle-tubing sleeve.

All of this reminds us that the US Army allegedly required twice as many CSRGs as originally planned. The reason often advanced is that the Doughboys threw them away at the first opportunity; and this apparently simplistic explanation should not be dismissed lightly. Consider the probable reactions of a soldier in the shell-blasted mud of the Western Front, burdened with a heavy (21lb - 9.5kg) and very cheaply-made weapon, which suddenly refuses to fire - or even to open, despite persuasion with a "size 10 brogan" (boot). No doubt a lot of American boys did indeed decide that their lives were worth more than an armful of clogged French plumbing.

Perhaps most telling is the apparent disdain of the Germans for captured Chauchats. While the highly prized Lewis was even included in the training course for Maxim gunners, there is no evidence that CSRGs were used in any organised way by the Kaiser's armies.

Squad organisation

Battle experience also showed the two-man team to be too overburdened by weapon and ammunition to effectively keep up with riflemen in the assault. Since "walking fire" in the offensive was supposed to be the very core of the CSRG's purpose this could not be tolerated. First, in July 1916, an additional ammo carrier was assigned to the crew; then, by October 1917, they had acquired a separate team leader.

In autumn 1917 the French Army radically reorganised the basic infantry element, giving the company 12 Chauchats, and the Chauchat gunner and his two carrier/assistants direct support from rifle grenadiers, hand grenadiers, and riflemen. The mission of this *demi-section de combat* ("half-platoon") was primarily to destroy the rapidly proliferating German MG 08/15 light machine gun crews. This was to be accomplished by fire from the four-man CSRG team keeping the heads of the enemy crew down until the long range, high angle fire of three men armed with Vivien-Bessiéres rifle grenade dischargers could silence the gun. One squad each of hand grenadiers and riflemen were available as needed, also carrying extra ammunition. By the Armistice of 1918 the standard platoon organisation was three *groupes de combat*, each consisting of one CSRG-and-rifle team and one bombing-and-rifle team - thus paralleling the evolution of minor tactics already seen in the German and British armies.

* * *

Despite severe criticism arising from both the "bugs" in initial production guns and the inevitable consequences of an imperfect design, there was no turning back. Due to the universal bureaucratic law - "It's the Best We Have Right Now and It Would Take Too Much Money and Time to Get Something Better" - production orders to Gladiator were increased to 155,000 guns. Anticipating the need not only to replace battle losses of guns and astounding numbers of magazines, but to provide additional automatic rifles to counter the German light machine gun build-up, a second manufacturer was engaged. In December 1916 another 25,000 Mle 1915 FMs were ordered from Forges et Aciéries de la Marine à Homecourt, a heavy ordnance factory at St.Chamond; these guns were distinctively marked on the left side of the receiver with a six-pointed star and the word SIDARME. Embarrassingly, the first of the St.Chamond production line guns are reported to have performed much better in full automatic sustained fire acceptance testing than the control guns provided by Gladiator. The need for ever greater production of both heavy and light machine guns was aggravated in 1917 by the knowledge that the American Expeditionary Force would soon be arriving in France suffering from a critical shortage of these weapons.

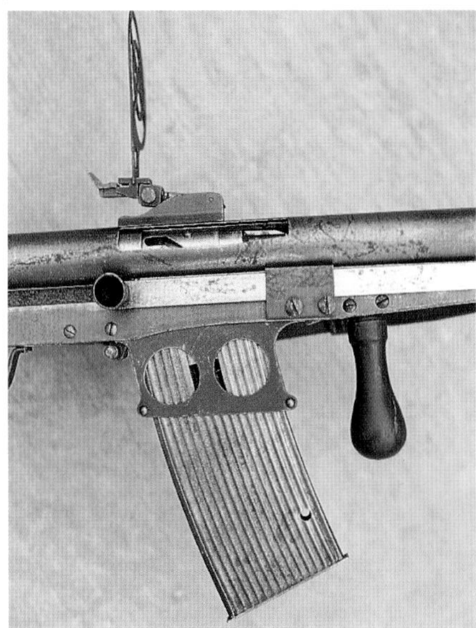

Right side of the receiver of the M1918 conversion with detail of magazine, magazine housing, and repositioned foregrip.

"The Yanks are Coming!"

"By May 1918 the first 12 divisions of American troops had reached France. They were all equipped with Hotchkiss heavy machine guns and Chauchat automatic rifles - both kinds supplied by the French government. During May and June, 11 American divisions sailed, and the heavy machine gun equipment of these troops was American built, consisting of Vickers guns. For their light machine guns these 11 divisions received the French Chauchat rifles in France. After June 1918 all American troops to sail were supplied with a full equipment of Browning guns, both of the light (M1918 BAR) and heavy (M1917) types." (Benedict Crowell, *America's Munitions 1917-18*, 1919)

When General "Black Jack" Pershing's American Expeditionary Force (AEF) arrived in France they brought with them little beyond uniforms, rifles and some

BELOW LEFT AND RIGHT *The V-notch tangent rear sight is marked in 200m increments from 200m to an absurdly optimistic 2,000m, and is offset to the left to accommodate the correct body position when firing.*

The sturdy front sight is permanently affixed to the barrel nut; proper "zero" can be attained by slight rotation of the nut using a large wrench.

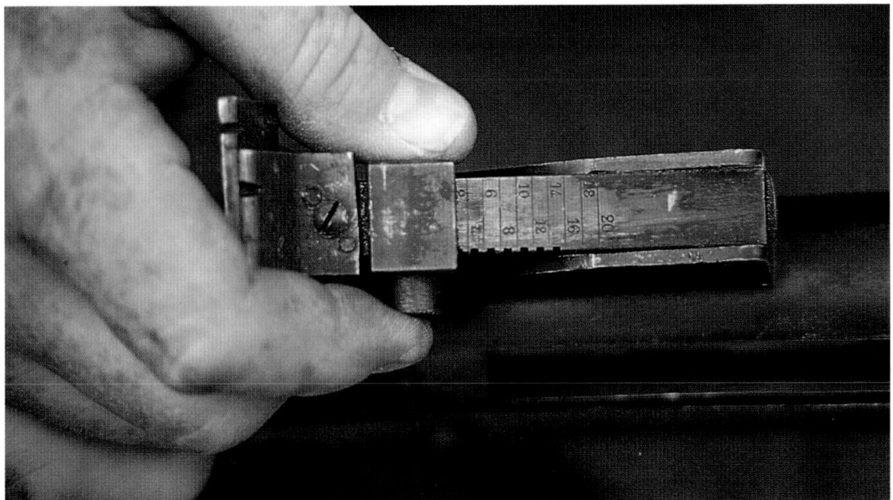

The fire selector is accessible only from the left side; its shallow detents sometimes fail to hold it in position when the gun brushes against the body. The illogical sequence of its arc seems unwise - from "S", safe, to "M", full automatic (mitrailleuse), *to "C", semi-automatic* (coup par coup).

rifle ammunition. The job of fully equipping and training the strong, confident, but green Americans fell upon seasoned British and French veterans of four years of trench warfare. Depending on which sector they were assigned, their host nations strove to integrate the "Yanks" or "Sammies" into their existing tactical and logistical structure.

It is not surprising that the Americans reportedly balked at the Chauchat (whose name they mangled phonetically into "Show-Show"). The CSRG looked remarkably crude compared to the Lewis guns they had left behind, and soon proved unreliable, inaccurate, heavy and poorly balanced. In one of the more puzzling episodes in the history of America's fighting men, newly-arrived US Marines were actually forced to give up their Lewis guns in exchange for Chauchats, ostensibly because of an acute shortage at the time of .30-06 ammunition, perhaps coupled with the need to foster a spirit of Allied co-operation.

Despite all the negative comments, "good" Chauchats are mentioned in the following and countless other citations for heroism in the Great War:

"At daylight the barrage lifted, but the fog and smoke obscured the view to the river. We could hear the Chauchats and rifles firing, the rattle of machine guns, and out of the fog and within a few yards of us before we could see them came men of Company B. They said the Germans were streaming across a pontoon bridge directly in front of us. Lieutenant Arthur S.Savage, a man among men, died at our end of the bridge, firing a Chauchat rifle after the gunners had been killed."
(Edmund L.Butts, *The Keypoint of the Marne*, 1930)

In Lawrence Stalling's *The Doughboys* it is reported that one Pte.Nels Wold of the US 35th Infantry Division used a Chauchat during the Meuse-Argonne offensive to take out four German machine gun positions, before being killed in an attempt to get the fifth. The same book records that a US Marine message runner named Frank Bart was recommended for the Medal of Honor after using a CSRG to kill two German machine gun crews who had stalled the advance of his entire company.

The conversion from Hell

When sufficient stocks of US .30-06 ammunition arrived from home, the decision was made to convert 8mm Chauchats to use the American cartridge. This would eliminate the need to supply two types of rifle and machine gun ammunition to the forward trenches. Requiring little more than substitution of a new barrel with the correct chamber and bore dimensions, it was optimistically considered a simple job, and Gladiator got the contract. The French C-shaped magazine was replaced with a more conventional rectangular box type holding 16 rounds; the foregrip was repositioned closer to the bipod; and the sights were recalibrated to conform to the new ballistics. This conversion was officially adopted by the US Army and Marine Corps as the "Caliber .30 Chauchat Automatic Rifle, Model of 1918."

The original French gun was designed and built to handle the relatively low-powered 8mm Lebel cartridge. Its long-recoil action was at least adequately served by easy extraction afforded by the steeply tapered case and thick, protruding rim of the Mle 1886 ammunition. In sharp contrast, the American .30-06 cartridge was much more powerful and correspondingly violent in recoil; the case is virtually parallel-sided, and the rim much thinner. These factors, combined with the gun's marginally adequate construction, almost guaranteed disaster.

France, 1918: a Mle 1915 CSRG rests against the sandbagged wall of a trench behind a resting pair of Doughboys. Note that the bolt and cocking handle are in the fully forward position - loaded, but safe and less susceptible to dirt getting inside. (USACMH)

When the Model 1918 was fired the barrel and bolt assembly were thrown backward with a force far exceeding that of its predecessor. After prolonged firing the converted guns would quickly jam due to overheating, or simply shake themselves apart. The long, straight sides of the American cartridge tended to stick to the chamber, causing the extractor to either break or tear right through the rim. Another problem with the M1918 guns has been brought to light by Demaison & Buffetaut (see Bibliography): it seems that many of the barrels supplied by an unknown subcontractor to Gladiator were incorrectly milled and reamed in the chamber. This and other instances of sloppy manufacture and inspection allowed significant quantities of fatally flawed guns to be issued to unsuspecting Doughboys.

While there are good reasons for despising the 8mm Chauchat, it is speculated that these bad .30cal. guns are the origin of much of the most intense derision that clings to its reputation even today. Most of the 18,000 .30cal. guns delivered to the AEF were junked, and only a handful are known to exist today. First issues of the far superior Model 1918 Browning Automatic Rifle were greeted with jubilation by American troops - and no wonder. . . .

Total wartime production of 8mm Chauchats is said to have been some 227,000 at Gladiator and 20,000 at St.Chamond. The weapon continued in French use until the adoption of the far superior Chatellerault FM Mle 1924. Surprisingly, surplus CSRGs were sometimes modified and pressed into service with the armies of Belgium, Greece, Poland and other nations between the World Wars.

Individual rounds are slipped base first into the magazine with one hand while the other slides the follower down. The sharply tapering 8mm Lebel cartridge dictated the semi-circular shape of the 20-round magazine - considerably short-loaded here, given its weak old spring. Although manuals specify that the bolt should be cocked and the safety engaged before loading, this allows dirt to enter the ejection port. Rain and battlefield filth also got in through the large open slots in the magazine - officially justified as allowing the assistant to judge the number of rounds remaining and to replace the magazine on the move during continuous "walking fire". The toe of the magazine is placed into the recess under the receiver, just behind the barrel catch block, and it is then rotated upward until it locks into its catch.

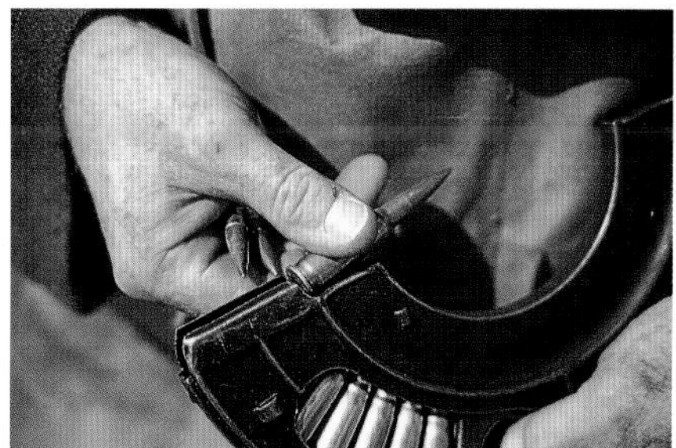

Chauchat Technical Specifications

Nomenclature	Fusil Mitrailleur Modèle 1915 CSRG
Manufacturer	Societé des Cycles Clement et Gladiator, Paris; Forges et Aciéries de la Marine à Homecourt, St.Chamond
Calibre	8mm Lebel Mle 1886D(am)
Ammunition	Ball; tracer
System of operation	Long recoil
Cooling	Air
Selector	Full and semi-automatic
Feed	20-round crescent-shaped detachable box magazine
Length	45ins (1143mm)
Weight	21lbs (9.5kg) w/loaded magazine
Barrel	17.5ins (55.8mm); 4 grooves, right twist
Sights	Post front; adjustable V-notch rear graduated from 200m-2,000m
Rate of fire	250rpm cyclic
Muzzle velocity	2,375fps (723mps)
Max.effective range	400m (point targets), 600m (area targets)

Cock the weapon by pulling the charging handle all the way to the rear, where it locks into position. Place the weapon on SAFE unless firing immediately.

Mechanism

There is often confusion over the difference between "recoil" and "blowback" systems of operation of self-loading weapons. In somewhat simplified terms: *blowback* is applicable to pistol calibre weapons only (e.g. the MP18/I), where an unlocked bolt of calculated weight is held in position by its mass and a recoil spring for long enough after detonation of the cartridge to get the bullet on its way, before their resistance is overcome by the backwards force of the detonation and the bolt is kicked back to pick up the next round. *Recoil* operation is more applicable to rifle calibre weapons (e.g. the Maxim and Vickers); the bolt is locked to the barrel, with both components mounted in a receiver which allows them to slide back together on detonation. At a predetermined point the bolt and barrel are uncoupled or unlocked by mechanical interruption. The Chauchat functions by *long recoil*, whereby the bolt and barrel travel backwards a greater distance than the full length of a loaded cartridge before unlocking; the bolt then stays to the rear as the barrel returns forward.

OPPOSITE BOTTOM *Attempting to fire the Chauchat. Although we tried several different magazines and applied a lot of WD-40 spray lubricant, the longest burst we were able to get off was about four rounds. After we found a tolerable magazine that would would not cause an immediate failure to feed, failure to extract was the most common stoppage.*

Cycle of operation

Once again, the inside workings of the CSRG are probably best described simply by quotation from Col.Chinn's classic *The Machine Gun, Vol.1*:

"To fire the Chauchat, a loaded magazine is inserted between the side plate and the bottom of the barrel. The rear end is then pushed up until the magazine catch snaps, holding it in position. To fire a single shot, the fire regulator is changed from 'S' (Sureté/safe) to 'C' (coup par coup/ semi-auto). If automatic fire is desired, the regulator is moved to 'M' (mitrailleuse/ machine gun).

"Assuming that automatic fire is desired and the regulator is properly set, the operating knob is pulled to the rear until the sear engages the notch in the feed piece holding the action in the cocked bolt position. Pulling the trigger rearward releases the operating mechanism, allowing it to fly forward under the energy of the compressed driving spring. The rolling action of the cocking assembly pushes a cartridge from the mouth of the magazine, where it is picked up by the bolt and chambering of the round begins. This action is assisted by the cartridge guide which cams the point of the bullet up into the entrance of the chamber. A cam then moves the guide out of the way of the magazine mouth.

"As the bolt travels forward, the locking lugs are vertical. To insure their remaining temporarily in this position, the bolt stop is used. This consists of a conical plug that fits partly in the bolt body and partly in the bolt head, thus preventing a torque motion between the two parts except when released. When the cartridge is firmly seated, the bolt stop rides inside the breech housing forcing the bolt head to turn. This locks the assembly securely when the movement forward has reached its limit. The driving spring continues to drive forward the portion of the bolt body that carries the striker, since the final rotary motion of the locking lugs frees the striker to detonate the primer.

"The bolt, barrel and barrel extension recoil rearward, still locked together, for a distance greater than the combined overall length of the cartridge case and bullet. At a point slightly less than its full rearward stroke, the bolt lugs unlock the bolt from the barrel extension and barrel. The bolt is then held to the rear by a searing device and the barrel extension and barrel start counter-recoil. As the rim of the fired cartridge is held secure in the extractor in the bolt face, the barrel and barrel extension, in starting forward to battery (full return), pull away from the spent brass. When the barrel has traveled a distance that will permit it, a spring-loaded ejector bearing on the empty case kicks it from the ejection slot in the right side of the receiver.

"It the trigger remains depressed, the barrel assembly cams the sear off just before it reaches battery, releasing the bolt that has been held to the rear, and the cycle is repeated."

BELOW *The 8mm Lebel Mle 1886 Balle D(am) - an aerodynamic "boat-tailed" 198-grain bullet pushed by 48 grains of smokeless powder. The almost wedge-shaped cartridge profile helped extraction, but the prominent rim posed serious feed problems. Although this particular gun lived up to the CSRG's generally poor reputation, at least some of the problems were due to the old ammunition we used during our first trial; this casing (bottom) shows a split neck, caused by brittle brass giving way on firing.*

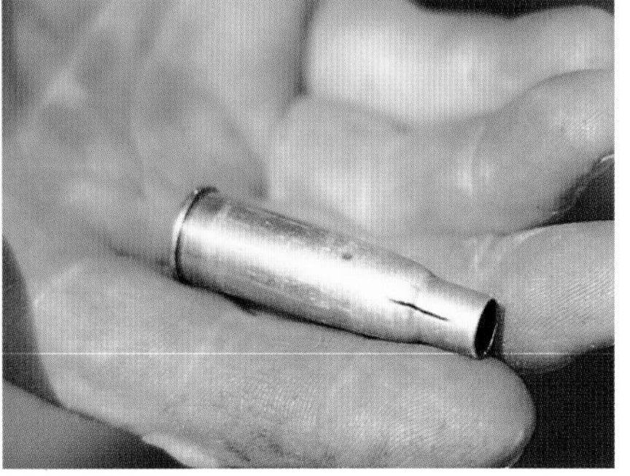

Firing the Chauchat

We had to conduct two sessions in order to get good action photos and a feel for the gun's performance; and our first was one of the most frustrating of the whole series conducted for this book. I have noted the declarations of collectors and enthusiasts who have lined up on opposite sides of the CSRG debate. Some state - in a tone of "believe it or not" - that they have, or know someone who swears he has, fired a Mle 1915 that functioned well.

The first session, with a gun owned Charles Erb - who contributed so much to the preparation of this book - was not one of our happier experiences. Despite extensive work with emery paper and various lubricants, and different combinations of ammunition and magazines, we could not persuade it to fire more than four rounds at a time, and usually only one or two.

When it did shoot, this Chauchat gave alarming new meaning to the word "uncontrollable." The barrel assembly and related parts have so far to move, and at such speed, that the whole gun bounces around on its flimsy bipod, causing the sights to make a jerky orbit around the target. Its sedate rate of fire, at four rounds per second (compared with e.g. the Lewis gun's ten rounds) should have made for exceptional controllability. Instead, each burst with the CSRG was like riding a bicycle with a solid front tire down a staircase - hold on for your life!

To be as fair as possible, we didn't at the time have the advantage of the original French training recommendations quoted in Demaison & Buffetaut's book. We did not know that the gunner's position should radically depart from the straight-behind-the-gun posture taught for virtually all other automatic rifles; and we had not appreciated that the painful bruising of the cheekbone from the receiver plug was so notorious that the effect had a recognised name. We had to learn the hard way.

France, 1918: a Doughboy poses wearing a German machine gunner's steel body armour. His Mle 1915 Chuachat leans against the sandbags, protected by a slip-on canvas cover. (NARA)

Abandoning for the time being any hope of an objective shooting test, we concentrated on other aspects of the weapon. Its human engineering, for example, seems to have been an afterthought. It is uncomfortable to carry; awkward to shoot from the hip; difficult to load and cock, and difficult to clear when the inevitable jams occur.

The simple **bipod** has legs which are not adjustable for length, but will fold up alongside the receiver. It pivots at the apex, allowing twisting of the receiver to

level the sights. While it is positioned well forward for stability in longer range shooting, it is not sturdy enough for consistent aiming from the prone position.

The open V-notch rear and sharp post front **sights** are a good choice for accurate target engagement under all light conditions. It would have been an improvement, however, to have the rear sight on a taller platform so that the gunner's neck does not have to be scrunched down to align them properly; and this would also minimise the "smack" in the face for unsuspecting novice gunners. The 2,000m maximum range setting would be amusing if the weapon's accuracy at anything beyond 400m were not so tragic. Sadly there is no provision for windage adjustment, as most guns reportedly shot high and to the right of the point of aim for the factory-set sights.

A whimsical accessory is the set of anti-aircraft sights. This clamp-on rear ring grid and front post are carried in the gunner's kit, ready for instant attachment should Boche flying machines venture too close. . . Has anyone ever found a citation for any aircraft ever being brought down by a CSRG?

The **pistol grip** is a rectangular slab of nearly unfinished wood riveted to the grip frame. While set at a moderate angle, it is uncomfortable to hold for any period of time. The trigger guard is large enough to allow access by a gloved finger and sturdy enough to protect the trigger from damage by rough handling. The **foregrip** is a pear-shaped "tool handle", located not for optimum support in standing and prone fire, but because the magazine is in the way of the balance point of the gun. Relocation of the foregrip on the US Model 1918 is perhaps that weapon's only good point.

After considerable work by gunsmith Charles Erb a second firing test was carried out, this time in the uniform of a 1918 poilu. On the move through the trenches, our gunner grasps the folded legs of the bipod with his left hand and the foregrip with the right; he should be using the sling over his left shoulder to help balance the load when carrying and to support the gun when assault firing.

This time full automatic fire was achieved; note the big Lebel empty ejecting to the right. Our gunner found that he had to hold the magazine in place with his left hand, positioning it a bit higher than the latch does, to aid feeding by bringing each round into a more direct line with the chamber as the bolt drove it forward. The position of his cheek, forward of the receiver plug, should save him from the worst of "the smack" - the bruising commonly suffered by CSRG gunners.

The large rectangular slot in the **receiver** behind the charging handle is an invitation to dirt when the gun is not cocked; and when it is, the large rectangular slot of the ejection port offers another entry for all kinds of undesirable foreign matter. A prototype set of metal protective covers was made in 1917 but, curiously, not adopted.

Perforations in the tubular steel **barrel shroud** theoretically allow better cooling of the ribbed aluminium barrel collar. In practice they act as yet more dirt ports, allowing entry of grit and moisture to retard movement of the recoiling parts. Being quite short at only 17.5ins the barrel requires a prominent **flash hider** at the muzzle because of incomplete combustion of propellant gas. Remarkably, this important piece of night firing equipment did not appear on factory guns until early 1917.

Magazine change is a troublesome procedure due to its half-moon configuration and its location. On the plus side, its release bar is quite well designed,

The "long recoil" action of the cycling parts makes for a remarkable degree of recoil movement in both directions when firing, seen here in the blurring of the gun and gunner; this is a serious impediment to accuracy. Even worse, the thin buttstock concentrates the kick painfully on a small area of the shoulder.

extending prominently from both sides and cleverly notched to serve as a catch-rest for the bipod legs when folded up alongside the receiver.

On the left side of the receiver the large **fire selector** is located above the pistol grip; the settings are described above in Chinn's passage. The **sling swivels** are well positioned on the left side, correctly angled for carry over the shoulder on the march and over the neck in assault fire.

"It's alive!. . ."

We had better luck during our second attempted gun test at the Shimpstown re-enactment site. Charles Erb was determined not to let the Chauchat get the better of him, and had torn the gun down and diagnosed the problem as possible incomplete machining of the chamber. After reaming and polishing, followed by a bit of deburring and general clean-up of the recoiling surfaces, the old French warhorse was persuaded to stir into life.

This time we were using late 1940s production 8mm Lebel ammunition which had been stored properly, and was up to the job of powering the notoriously balky action. However, the old curse of the magazines was still with us; for uninterrupted feed it became necessary to push the mag up with one hand from underneath, or to rest the gun on the magazine - a real tactical sin. Still, it worked; and the Chauchat *pup-pup-pupped* away for the photo sequences shown here.

Maximum range was limited for safety reasons to 150m - only about 100 meters short of the effective maximum for full automatic fire at point targets. For best control we started in the prone, bipod-supported position. True to form, with the sights carefully aligned on a cardboard Boche, the point of impact of the bursts was high and to the right. It took a couple more bursts to get the bullets onto the target. Predictably, semi-auto shots were more effective, despite the lunging of the gun as the cycling parts slam forward.

Further firing was conducted from a sitting position with the muzzle resting inside a trench loop-hole; then Erb got up and went "over the top" for some standing hip fire. Tracers would have helped immensely, but would not have been historically accurate. Our gunner did his best to keep the intermittent stream of short bursts on the silhouette despite the front-heavy gun and its highly energetic recoil stroke.

Firing the CSRG through a trench loophole; in static defence, with time for careful preparation and frequent cleaning, some of the gun's worst drawbacks could be countered more effectively than in the bullet-lashed confusion of a running fight among the shellholes of No Man's Land.

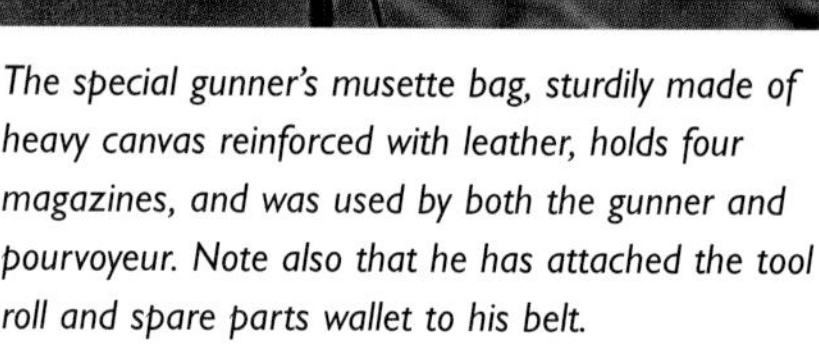

The special gunner's musette bag, sturdily made of heavy canvas reinforced with leather, holds four magazines, and was used by both the gunner and pourvoyeur. Note also that he has attached the tool roll and spare parts wallet to his belt.

The correct assault fire stance with the Mle 1915 requires the buttstock to be held firmly against the body with the elbow, but the left hand should be on the wooden knob foregrip - without the support of a sling this makes for a thoroughly unbalanced, front-heavy grip. Here the gunner is holding on forward of the magazine in an attempt to balance the weapon: this can lead to painful burns after a couple of mags in rapid fire.

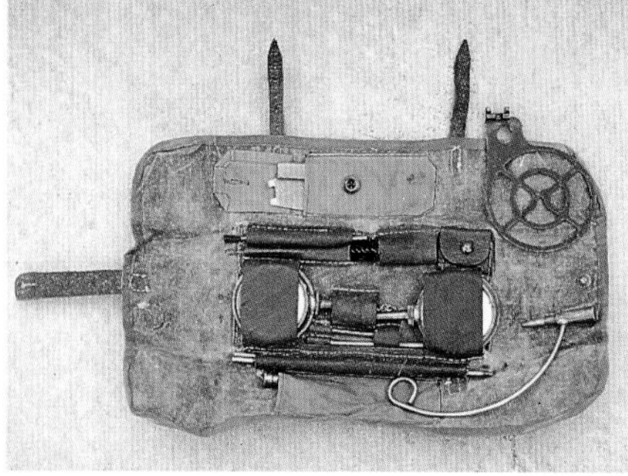

The essential canvas and leather gunner's wallet contains many of the tools necessary to keep the CSRG in firing order. According to the 1917 US manual it contained: three-piece cleaning rod, barrel cleaning brush, oil can, kerosene can, hand ejector, barrel sleeve swab, barrel nut scraper, cleaning swab, and M1907 broken case extractor. Other items pictured include AA sights, and a magazine checking tool (dummy cartridge on a wire).

Conclusion

Demaison and others have advanced the CSRG as the first practical version of what was to become today's ubiquitous "assault rifle". This contention is supported by the use of stamped sheet metal in its construction, its selective fire capability, pistol grip, detachable high-capacity magazine, and straight-line configuration. The important gap in this list is the absence of an intermediate calibre round: a lower powered *"petit Lebel"* cartridge was never invented.

Theoretical speculation aside, the fact remains that the CSRG fell far short of the demands made by the tactical doctrine which gave it birth. The design was an inadequate response to the realities of the battlefield; the innovative industrial means selected for its construction proved sadly immature; in many respects the Chauchat was "user-hostile", and in some positively dangerous.

Credits

Gun owner & French gunner, Charles Erb, Fredericktown, PA; AEF gunner, Murray S.Bayer, Canonsburg, PA; uniforms & equipment, National Capitol Historical Sales, Springfield, VA, Butch Fogel & Brian Pohanka, Alexandria, VA; location assistant, John Exley IV, Mechanicsville, VA; range, Great War Association, Shimpstown, PA. Primary research source: Demaison, Gerard, & Buffetaut, Yves, *Honour Bound*.

STRIPPING THE CHAUCHAT

Remove the magazine; check the chamber to ensure that no round is present; hold the cocking handle and pull the trigger, allowing the bolt to ride forward.

Push down on the spring-guide latch and unscrew the spring guide tube.

Remove the barrel recoil spring and guide tube assembly.

Lift the muzzle, and the recoil spring bushing will drop out.

Withdraw the rear assembly bolt.

Disengage the front assembly bolt by giving it a quarter-turn downward; this partially frees the two main groups.

Pull the cocking handle to the rear, allowing the barrel sleeve group to be moved further rearward and separated as the feed piece cam slides out from its cover.

Pull the cocking handle even further to the rear so that the feed piece can be removed from a slot in the breech casing.

The bolt and the barrel can now be removed through the rear of the barrel sleeve.

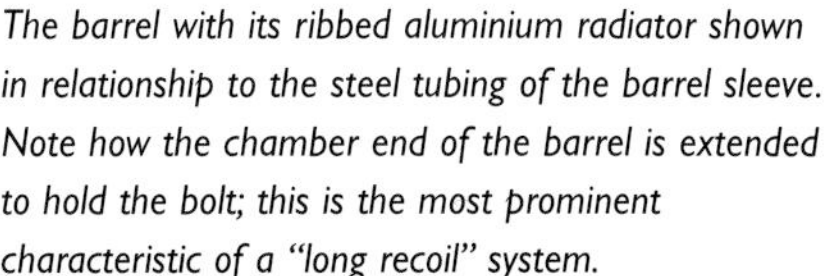

The barrel with its ribbed aluminium radiator shown in relationship to the steel tubing of the barrel sleeve. Note how the chamber end of the barrel is extended to hold the bolt; this is the most prominent characteristic of a "long recoil" system.

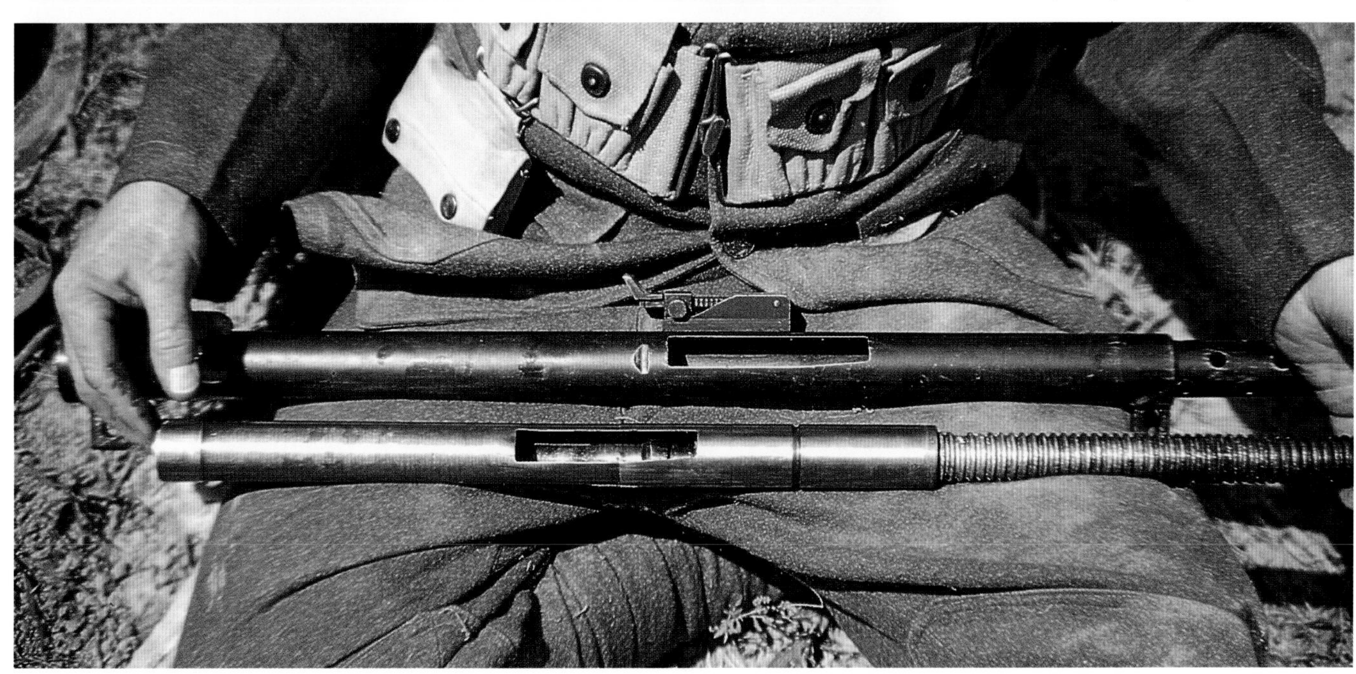

Field strip layout (top to bottom, left to right):
Receiver group; barrel sleeve; recoil spring bushing; barrel; feed piece cam; recoil spring guide tube assembly; rear assembly bolt; magazine; bolt.

Relationship of the bolt face with the rimmed base of an 8mm cartridge. Note the extractor at 7 o'clock, the ejector at 2 o'clock, and the thick locking lugs at 3 and 9 o'clock.

AFTERWORD: Machine Guns between the World Wars

Browning .50cal. water-cooled heavy machine gun. The French 11mm Hotchkiss "balloon gun" inspired parallel development in America and Germany of 13mm cartridges to dramatically increase the range, armour penetration and destructive effect of machine guns. Although not completed until after the Great War, the Browning .50cal. quickly set the world standard for heavy machine guns and - in its more familiar air-cooled M2 version - still does. The gun pictured here has AA sights and a convertible tripod cradle set up for AA use. (Colts Patent Firearms Co.)

"There was a second of silence from the enemy . . . . Then, suddenly, their machine gun fire burst out in nervous spasms and splashed the sides of 'Creme de Menthe.' But the tank did not mind. The bullets fell from its sides, harmlessly. It advanced upon a broken wall, leaned up against it heavily until it fell with a crash of bricks, and then rose on to the bricks and passed over them, and walked straight into the midst of the factory ruins.

"From its sides came flashes of fire and a hose of bullets, and then it trampled around over machine gun emplacements, 'having a grand time' as one of the men said with enthusiasm. It crushed the machine guns under its heavy ribs, and killed machine gun teams with a deadly fire. The infantry followed in and took the place after this good help, and then advanced again round the flanks of the monster." (Philip Gibbs, *The Battles of the Somme*)

The first slow, unreliable generation of tanks were in fact far from invulnerable; but in 1918 it was they - together with advances in both artillery and infantry tactics - which helped break up the frozen nightmare of trench warfare by carrying light cannon and machine gun crews safely across No Man's Land into the German positions. But the infantry machine gun was never to lose the central place in warfare which it had so dreadfully earned between 1914 and 1918. The aftermath of the Great War saw some empires crumble, others expand, with the inevitable consequences of civil war and revolution. Newspapers and newsreels from all over the world would soon show the Maxim, Vickers and Hotchkiss back in action; and in the major industrial powers inventors continued to advance the science of machine-gunnery.

The **Maxim** soldiered on in postwar Germany and elsewhere, most notably with the Russian armies. An early customer of Vickers Sons & Maxim, Russia had soon begun to make guns under license in the state arsenal at Tula. They remained in Red Army service, essentially unchanged, until after the end of World War II; the production total is estimated at some 600,000 guns. Hundreds of thousands more Maxims have been made by the Chinese, as well as untold numbers of other commercial and license-built guns for many countries.

It is unsurprising that the German Army, its postwar numbers limited by the Versailles Treaty, turned to technical ingenuity to multiply its fighting potential for the future. The unsatisfactory MG08/15 was a prime candidate for replacement in the quest for a "universal machine gun"; and the whole body of experimentation with air cooling and quick-change barrels came together in the MG34. Combining the best of each class of machine gun into a simple, light and efficient package, it began a revolution in design that would eventually lead to total abandonment of water-cooled guns by the world's armies.

The evolutionary pace of **Vickers** development picked up in the 1930s with

Germany, January 1919: US Army .30cal. Browning M1917 water-cooled machine gun on the firing range. Measurably superior to similar guns of the period, John Browning's simple and reliable weapon arrived too late to have a significant effect in the closing months of the World War, but would remain in service for many years. (NARA)

Hawaii, 1939: men of a US Navy landing force demonstrate the .30-06 calibre Lewis, retained by the USN until well into World War II. Note wooden chest for six magazines. (NARA)

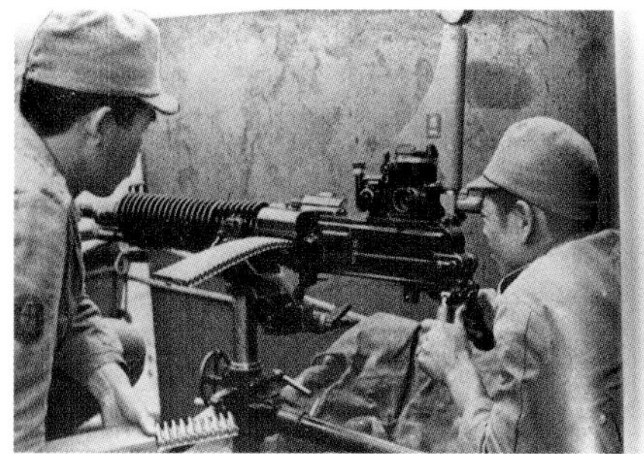

Pacific, c.1944: inside a concrete pillbox a Japanese gunner sights through an optical periscope mounted on his 7.7mm Type 92 heavy machine gun, the most widely used Japanese gun of its class. Based on the Hotchkiss system, it was nicknamed the "wood pecker" by US troops from its distinctive sound. (USACMH)

further refinements in the gun and new ancillaries, particularly in the area of sights and fire control. Before World War II a new nitrocellulose-loaded Mk VIIIZ cartridge was introduced, featuring an aerodynamic, boat-tailed, 175-grain bullet and far outranging the old cordite-loaded Mk VII, extending the indirect reach of the Vickers from 3,500 to an astounding 4,500 yards - two and a half miles. Its punishing recoil made the Mk VIIIZ unsuitable for use in the rifle and new Bren light machine gun, and it was fired exclusively from the tough old Vickers, which continued to serve the British, Commonwealth, and many other forces with distinction for many decades. The British Army finally replaced it from 1964 with the L7A1, a license-built sustained fire version of the Belgian MAG58.

After the Great War the French Army concentrated small arms development on a light machine gun, the Chatellerault FM24/29, and on a new rifle, the MAS36. Unlike the Chauchat - replaced by the FM24 series as soon as it was available - the Mle 1914 **Hotchkiss** was highly enough regarded to remain in service until the end of World War II. It even soldiered on in Indochina in 1946-54 for lack of sufficient numbers of modern US types, and quantities were captured by the Communist insurgent armies - many being turned later against the South Vietnamese and Americans.

Lewis guns served on in the US and various European armies for many years following 1918. Along with the Browning Automatic Rifle, they were still in first line service with many US Navy, Marine Corps and Army units in the early years of World War II. In the mid-1930s the British Army replaced most of their Lewis guns in the infantry role with the excellent Czech-designed Bren gun; but in secondary roles - e.g. in anti-aircraft, vehicle and naval mountings, and with the Home Guard - the Lewis remained in action throughout the war. Indeed, following the disaster in France in May-June 1940 thousands of American ground and aircraft model Lewis guns were "Lend-Leased" to Britain to make up the shortfall in machine guns.

License for production of the Lewis aircraft model was purchased for the rapidly expanding Japanese Navy and its air arm during the mid-1920s. Manufactured to accept the 7.7mm Type 92 rimmed copy of the British .303in cartridge, these weapons were variously identified as the Model 1929, 1932 and Navy Type 92, and all served throughout World War II. The Lewis was also used in quantity for varying periods by the forces of France, Holland, Norway, Russia, Portugal, Italy and many other nations; its bolt and camming gas piston/carrier system was later adopted by Rheinmetall for the German FG42 paratroop machine rifle, and serves on even today in the US Army's M60 general purpose machine gun.

Although it appeared only at the very end of World War I, John Moses Browning's Model 1917 .30cal. water-cooled machine gun was quickly recognised as superior in many ways to comparable heavy machine guns then in use. Over the next 60 years and more this tough and reliable short-recoil weapon outperformed all others on land, sea and in the air. Browning's massive .50cal.(12.7mm) water- and air-cooled guns, perfected in the mid-1920s, were particularly successful; and the air-cooled version is still in first-line service with the US and many other armies.

Doughboys give a live fire demonstration of the US Army's new M1918 Browning Automatic Rifle near Washington, DC, in 1918; in both appearance and function it was a huge step forward from the Chauchat still used by the AEF until the Armistice, and an advance on the Lewis, which it replaced in US Army service in 1918 and in the US Marines in the 1930s. Note how the French doctrine of "walking fire" is being demonstrated, with a shoulder sling and the buttstock lodged in a metal cup on the gunner's belt. No.2 carries 12 additional magazines in six pouches on a special belt. (NARA)

Automatic rifles & sub-machine guns

The shortcomings of the Chauchat and the limitations of the Lewis also spurred Browning to build his Browning Automatic Rifle (BAR), adopted in 1918. This excellent weapon had an immediate impact on contemporary designers, and served in the US Army and Marine Corps until the late 1950s; it is still to be seen in Third World armies.

The honours for best postwar automatic rifle have to go to the Czech ZB26, which is best known in its British form as the Bren. With a bolt-locking system inspired by the BAR, a quick-change barrel and a handy magazine feed, it was a highly reliable and versatile weapon. Although Britain officially replaced the Bren (rechambered postwar for NATO 7.62mm ammunition as the L4A2) in the early 1960s with the bipod version of the belt-fed L7A1, the lighter, handier and more accurate Bren may even now be seen carried in occasional photos of out-of-area deployments by spearhead forces.

Some of the most dramatic developments in interwar small arms were in the class of sub-machine guns, founded by the German **MP18**. The Maschinenpistole concept was refined and improved in Germany through a series of designs, culminating in the mass-produced MP38 and MP40. The Italians moved ahead with the Beretta Modelo 1918 and 1938. The British Royal Navy issued the Lanchester, a copy of the German MP28 - itself derived from the MP18. The best-known sub-machine gun to emerge in the interwar years, however, was that developed by Payne & Eickhoff in the USA in 1917-18 and named after Gen.John T.Thompson. Originally intended as a "trench broom" in the manner of the German MP18, it fired the considerably more powerful .45 ACP cartridge. It soon saw action in various "small wars"; and so infamous did it become in the hands of gangsters in the 1920s-30s that "Tommy gun" remained a generic term for sub-machine guns for decades afterwards. In a more honourable cause the Thompson was the most widely used gun of its class in the armouries of the British Commonwealth and US forces throughout the first half of World War II, and remained in American service until after the Korean War.

* * *

Readers interested in learning more about the influence of the guns described in this book on some of the most famous automatic weapons of World War II are directed to the author's first title in this **Live Firing** series: **German Automatic Weapons of World War II** (Windrow & Greene, April 1997).

Seen here on an AA mount is the highly regarded Czech ZB26 light machine gun/ automatic rifle, adopted by the British Army in modified form as the Bren gun. Its sustained fire capability was not equal to that of the German MG34 and MG42, with their superior tripod mounts, so it cannot be classed as a true "universal machine gun"; but the Bren was light, accurate, reliable, and easy to handle as the infantry section's light automatic. (NARA)

LEFT *Texas, September 1942: a US Army corporal conducts a class on the M1928A1 Thompson sub-machine gun with 50-round drum magazine and Cutts muzzle compensator. (NARA)*

BELOW *1923 publicity shot of the M1923 Thompson with its distinctive 14in barrel and bipod. Although the 230-grain .45in bullet was devastating relative to the 9mm used by most sub-machine guns, the Thompson did not have sufficient effective range to be taken up in the light machine gun role.*

Select Bibliography
Author's note:

Readers who wish to know more about the hobby of World War I re-enactment and other aspects of the Great War should visit the informative Internet web site: *http://www.greatwar.com*
Or, in the USA, contact:
Great War Militaria, PO Box 552, Chambersburg, PA 17201,
telephone 717-264-6834, fax 717-267-1943

Modern & reprinted reference sources:

Armstrong, D.A., *Bullets and Bureaucrats*, Greenwood Press, Westport, CT, & London (1982)

Chinn, George M., *The Machine Gun, Vol.1*, US Dept. of the Navy, Bureau of Ordnance (1951); reprinted Edwards Brothers, Ann Arbor, MI

Crutchley, C.E., *Machine Gunner 1914-18*, Machine Gun Corps Old Comrades' Association, Northampton, England (1973)

Demaison, Gerard & Buffetaut, Yves, *Honour Bound - The Chauchat Machine Rifle*, Collector Grade Publications, Cobourg, Ontario, Canada (1995)

Goldsmith, D.L., *The Devil's Paintbrush*, Collector Grade Publications, Cobourg, Ontario, Canada (1989)

Goldsmith, D.L., *The Grand Old Lady of No Man's Land - The Vickers Machine Gun*, Collector Grade Publications, Cobourg, Ontario, Canada (1994)

Junger, Ernst, *The Storm of Steel*, Chatto & Windus, London (1929); reprinted Howard Fertig Publishing, New York (1975)

McBride, Herbert, *The Emma Gees*, Bobbs-Merrill, New York (1918), reprinted Lancer Militaria, Mt.Ida, AR

McBride, Herbert, *A Rifleman Went to War*, Small Arms Technical Publishing, Marines, NC (1935), reprinted Lancer Militaria, Mt.Ida, AR

Musgrave, Daniel D., *German Machineguns*, Ironside International, Alexandria, VA (1992)

Nelson, Thomas B. & Lockhoven, Hans B., *The World's Submachine Guns (Machine Pistols) Vol.I (1915-1963)*, TBN Enterprises (now Ironside International Publishers), Alexandria, VA (1963)

Truby, J.D., *The Lewis Gun*, Paladin Press, Boulder, CO (1976)

Old & out-of-print reference sources:

Anon., *Machine Gun Notes*, Army War College, Washington, DC (1917)

Applin, R.V.K., *Machine Gun Tactics*, Hugh Rees Ltd, London (1915)

Bond, P.S., *The ROTC Manual - Infantry, 1st Year Advanced, Vol.III*, National Service Publishing Co., Annapolis, MD (1925); and Military Service Publishing Co., Harrisburg, PA (1935)

Butts, E.L., *The Keypoint of the Marne*, Geo. Banta, Menasha, Wisconsin (1930)

Crozier, William, *Ordnance and the World War*, Chas.Scribner's Sons, New York (1920)

Empey, A.G., *Over The Top*, G.P.Putnam's Sons, London and New York (1917)

Gibbs, Philip, *The Battles of the Somme*, A.L.Burt Co., New York (1917)

Hatcher, J.S.(et al), *Machine Guns*, Geo.Banta, Menasha, Wisconsin (1917)

Hutchison, G.S., *Machine Guns - Their History and Tactical Employment*, McMillan & Co., London (1938)

Lafond, Georges, *Covered with Mud and Glory*, Small, Maynard & Co., Boston, MA (1918)

Longstaff, F.V. & Atteridge, A.H., *Book of the Machine Gun*, Dodd, Mead & Co., New York (1917)

Ludendorff, Erich, *Ludendorff's Own Story*, Harper & Bros., New York (1922)

Minder, Chas., *This Man's War*, Pevensey Press, New York (1931)

Solano, E.J., *Machine Gun Training*, George Harvey, New York (1917)